Second Generation DMUs

Title Page: *South West Trains Class 159/0 No 159012 crosses Blachford Viaduct near Ivybridge in Devon on 14 July 2005 forming the 14.47 Plymouth to London Waterloo via Exeter service.* **Author**

Above *A ten-car formation of Class 180 or 'Adelante' stock, which many describe as the most handsome of modern DMU types, crosses Cockwood Harbour between Exeter and Newton Abbot on 4 August 2004 when set Nos 180103 and 180108 formed the 14.35 Paddington to Plymouth service.* **Author**

Second Generation DMUs

Colin J. Marsden

Ian Allan
PUBLISHING

Contents

First published 2009

ISBN 978 0 86093 624 4

Published by Oxford Publishing Co
an imprint of Ian Allan Publishing Ltd, Hersham, Surrey KT12 4RG.

Printed in England by Ian Allan Printing Ltd, Hersham, Surrey KT12 4RG.

Code: 0901/B2

Visit the Ian Allan Publishing website at www.ianallanpublishing.com

Second Generation DMUs

Introduction

Welcome to *Second Generation DMUs*. A few years ago I would have been surprised to find such a title even considered for publication, the general opinion being that these new modern bus-like creatures operating the boring and mundane secondary passenger services would have no following at all.

However, today the story is quite different and most of these classes have a significant following among railway observers and photographers. While not possessing the glamour of a locomotive-powered train, the humble second-generation DMU has come in a variety of types, colours and many classes, having seen troublesome times, have even been rebuilt into other types.

The story of the second generation of UK DMU emerged when the British Railways Board had to plan ahead in the 1970s for the retirement of huge numbers of first generation DMU vehicles, with several hundred vehicles all coming up for replacement at around the same time.

Travelling requirements and the types of service needed had changed significantly since dieselisation of the secondary routes in the 1950s and purpose-designed lightweight rural trains were projected for the lesser-used and lightly-patronised lines - for this the Railbus project was born. However, for the longer-distance secondary routes a train more in keeping with an InterCity type express was sought, offering greater comfort levels, a mix of first and standard class seating and even such luxuries as air conditioning. For this the Sprinter range of DMUs was developed.

Following experience and a general customer dislike for the railbus type vehicles the rail industry concentrated further orders on more heavyweight designs. However the vast majority of these lightweight Railbus units are still in service in 2009.

In the years around privatisation the DMU story moved ahead quickly, with the birth in the immediate pre-privatisation period of several quality DMU products such as the Class 158, 159, 165 and 166.

In the privatisation years, with lease companies now owning trains rather than operators, no new train orders were placed for several years due to uncertainties in the industry; thankfully this was resolved in the post-privatisation period and classes such as the 168 and 170 Adtranz/Bombardier 'Turbostar' product range revolutionised rail travel.

Privatisation also brought about mass introduction of long-distance DMU-type trains for Virgin Trains on its CrossCountry Network with Bombardier Transportation building large fleets of tilt and non-tilt 'Voyager' trains; this was followed by similar orders for other train operators.

It sometimes seems hard to realise but after three years of rail privatisation more new trains were being delivered each month than ever before, with every part of the rail network benefiting, some from direct new trains and others from cascaded stock.

Not all the designs of 'new' train have been successful, as will be seen and discussed in the pages of this book.

As author, I would like to thank the many people from within the rail industry for assistance given during the production of this title, and also the the many photographers who have allowed me to include images from their collections.

All it leaves me to say is that I hope you enjoy reading and browsing the pages of *Second Generation DMUs* as much as I have enjoyed compiling the product.

Colin J. Marsden
Dawlish
November 2008

Below: *Following rebuild by Hunslet-Barclay of Kilmarnock, set No 141111 is seen parked at Sheffield, painted in Metro Train maroon and buttermilk livery.* **Author**

During the early to mid-1970s considerable work was being undertaken by the BRB design office on the next generation of diesel multiple-unit. The modernisation of the 1950s was wonderful at the time, but the near-complete replacement of the railways' short- to medium-haul trains in a few years in the late 1950s was to generate its own problems around 30 years on, when some 75 per cent of rural, local and outer suburban services operated by diesel multiple-unit trains would fall due for replacement at the same time.

As discussed in a subsequent chapter, main developments in the 1970s were in connection with the Class 210 DEMU project. However, in 1977-78 a group was set up at the Railway Technical Centre, Derby under the direction of the DM&EE to investigate rail carriage body design. The group was known as the 'Alternative Technology Project'. This began in conditions of some secrecy, not surprising as it was based upon the idea of using a bus body mounted on a railway underframe, with the vehicle interior laid out in bus style.

This project is a joint venture between BR Research and Leyland Bus. The idea was sound both at drawing board level and financially, as the Leyland National bus was used by many operators, the bodies being mass-produced on a modular basis in Workington.

The comparative cost of this type of vehicle superstructure against that of a typical railway-designed and built railcar or carriage was sufficiently different to offer significant financial savings.

The project was furthered, as a four-wheeled vehicle chassis had already been proved to ride safely and relatively smoothly at speed; this was the subject of part of Advanced Passenger Train (APT) development work already undertaken by BR Research at Derby.

Selling the idea of using bus technology to the railway trade unions was another problem, let alone the passengers. At one time it was minuted that consideration was given to employing the train operator to drive the vehicle, work the doors and sell tickets, just like a street bus. Indeed one early drawing showed the driving position set back from the vehicle end, inward from the doors with a counter and ticket machine on the driver's right side!

The design of joining a bus body to a rail underframe produced the Leyland Experimental Vehicle or LEV. Extensive proving of the project had to be undertaken and various bus body sections were fabricated at Workington and shipped to the Engineering Development Unit (EDU) at Derby; initially a non-powered short underframe four-wheeled trailer with bus-type driving cabs at each end was put together. This was first seen by the public and the railway press in June 1978, when the Advanced Passenger Train - pre-production prototype APT-P was shown to the press. The unpowered LEV was parked in the yard and generated as much if not more interest than the APT. Until then the far less sensational 'Alternative Technology' project, now renamed the LEV project, was unheard of and quite naturally attracted much attention.

Once a full rail/bus vehicle had been assembled, exhaustive static testing was carried out at Derby; this included the fitting of different front-end designs, side skirts and internal divisions, but no power equipment or brakes. After several months the vehicle was taken onto the main line, marshalled between two BR Research coaches to perform loco-hauled riding tests. These were carried out in and around Derby and then over the West Coast Main Line to Carlisle. Speeds of up to 60mph were achieved and the shell demonstrated its stability.

In 1979 an actual demonstration vehicle was assembled at the EDU; this had a slightly different body style, was a little longer and only had one pair of folding passenger doors on each side. It was also powered, using an underfloor engine with mechanical transmission and was fitted with brakes for service trials.

LEV1, also allocated the departmental number RDB975874, operated some initial test runs in the UK, mainly on Anglia branch lines in the Saxmundham area and on the Ipswich-Lowestoft line. Once these had been carried out to establish performance, LEV1 was exported to the United States of America, operating in the New Hampshire and Massachusetts area on the section between Lowell and Nashua for the New Hampshire Commuter Rail project. It was hoped that export orders for the design could be obtained through BR's Marketing arm, Transmark, but sadly nothing materialised.

Below: *The marrying together of two basic Leyland National bus bodies back-to-back to form a pre-production 'Alternative Technology' rail passenger vehicle took place at the Leyland factory in Workington in late 1977. Here the complete body structure is seen in the works yard awaiting road transfer to the Railway Technical Centre, Derby.* **Author's Collection**

LEV1 was eventually returned to the UK and used by the BR Research & Development team at Derby for several years; it did venture out onto the main line at times and was also recorded working over the two test tracks at Mickleover and Old Dalby. As LEV1 was of considerable interest in the history of British railways it was claimed by the National Railway Museum, but as the site did not have room to display the item as a permanent exhibit, it was stored, firstly in the depot yard and then inside the annexe, before being placed on long-term loan to the North Norfolk Railway, where it remains today.

The use of LEV1 in the USA did generate an amount of interest, sufficient for the Federal Railroad Administration (FRA) to order its own LEV. This vehicle became known as LEV2. It was built to a different design and incorporated Leyland bus components but was assembled by D. Wickham at their factory in Ware, Hertfordshire. Upon completion the vehicle was transferred to the BR Research lab in Derby and subsequently to the BR test track at Old Dalby.

LEV2 was a distinct advance upon the first vehicle, conforming to the requirements of the FRA. It went into trial service on the Boston & Maine Railroad in 1980, and operated between Concord, New Hampshire

Above: *Once at the RTC Derby the vehicle was finished off in the Engineering Development Unit building, where the structure was mounted on what was basically a high-speed freight vehicle chassis. This rare view shows the nose cone (never carried in traffic) and between-wheels skirt. Many trial fittings were made to the structure before static and limited dynamic tests were carried out to establish rigidity.* **Author's Collection**

Below: *To allow dynamic testing on the main line the vehicle structure was weighted and then rigidly coupled to two test cars. The basic shell is seen outside the EDU awaiting departure for Carlisle.* **Author's Collection**

Second Generation DMUs

Left: *The production Leyland Experimental Vehicle 1 (LEV1) was, after assembly at the RTC Derby, subjected to static testing before carrying out dynamic tests on the BR Research Old Dalby test track. Here, isolated from the national network, hundreds of miles of performance and ride-quality running were achieved. In early structural form without the air-smoothed casing over the route indicator area, LEV1 is seen about to enter Stanton Tunnel during early ride instrumentation trials and before mesh was fitted over the front windows.* **Author's Collection**

Below: *Although fitted with its own red rear marker lights, a standard BR oil tail light was carried to conform with rules and regulations. Here during a press trip from Derby to Matlock, LEV1 awaits the right away from Cromford on the outward journey on 30 May 1980. By the time this shot was taken mesh had been fitted to protect the driver and passengers from objects thrown from overbridges.* **Author's Collection**

and Lowell, Massachusetts, but sadly its light weight was to be its downfall; after only a short time in service it was in a serious collision with a road vehicle on a grade crossing. The cause was due to the light weight of the rail vehicle failing to activate the crossing controls. After months in store the FRA sold LEV2 to Amtrak, after another short period of use on the Northeast Corridor it was again involved in a grade crossing collision and subsequently withdrawn. Amtrak donated it to the Steamtown National Historic Site, who eventually sold it to a scrap dealer. Thankfully it was saved from disposal by the Durbin & Greenbrier Valley Railroad and later transferred to New England and its current home, the Connecticut Trolley Museum.

Back in the UK, lightweight rail vehicle technology was progressing and British Rail Engineering Ltd (BREL) and Leyland Bus agreed to proceed with another prototype, mainly due to the favourable reactions gained by LEV1. It was decided to exploit the export market with a joint product known as the BRE-Leyland Railbus. This was designed as a single unit, fully bi-directional and self-propelled, which could be adapted to multiple-unit operation if desired.

This third vehicle in the Railbus story became 'R3'. Publicity material of the day shows that this vehicle could carry 104 passengers (64 seated and 40 standing) and that the vehicle ends were now designed to withstand a compression load of 100 tonnes at coupling height. This last factor was of

considerable importance in the development story of the Railbus, as it did not match the BR specifications which at the time were developing to favour a two-car version of the design. This was of course the genesis of the Class 140 project.

Returning to R3, this vehicle was assembled at BREL Derby Litchurch Lane Works from body sections provided by Leyland and emerged in April 1981. It was finished in a stunning white, green and orange livery with full yellow warning ends. On the bodyside was the branding BRE-Leyland Railbus, with a joint BR/Leyland logo. After performing static tests at Litchurch Lane, the vehicle passed to the RTC for dynamic testing, this was performed on the Old Dalby test track as well as on the

Above: *Subsequent to its operations in the USA and many trials and demonstration runs in the UK, LEV1 was used by BR Research for various trials. On 30 September 1985 the vehicle is seen out of use parked in the yard of Derby Litchurch Lane Carriage Works.* **Author**

Left and Below: *After arrival in the USA for demonstration and testing LEV 1 was operated in the New Hampshire and Massachusetts area on the section of line between Lowell and Nashua on the New Hampshire Commuter Rail project. Reaction to the single vehicle was mixed, with people viewing the vehicle as 'small' (well, it was, compared to the much more generous US loading gauge). Seating was also criticised; again; this is not surprising, as the seats were identical to Leyland National bus seats. On the left, LEV1 is seen at Lowell collecting passengers for a demonstration run to Nashua. The view below shows LEV1 at the Boston North terminal.* **Author's Collection**

main line.

In October 1981 the vehicle became passenger registered as departmental No RDB977020 and was allocated to Bristol St Philips Marsh for use on the Bristol to Severn Beach line, a route on which it worked until June 1982. Booked to operate daily, it tended to work only a few days each week due to various problems and ongoing tests. On 25 April 1982 the vehicle was one of the exhibits at Laira Open Day, working between Bristol and Plymouth under its own power. This was one of the few occasions in the UK that saw passengers transported in a departmental-registered vehicle.

After returning to Derby in mid-1982, LEV3 was sold to Northern Ireland Railways later the same year,. It was then re-gauged from 4ft 8½in to 5ft 3in and deployed on the Coleraine to Portrush line, where it operated for around eight years. In 1990 the vehicle was taken out of service as its size could not

Left: *As the Railbus project progressed some interest was shown in squadron development; although nothing ever came of it, a full size twin-cabbed body shell was supplied by Leyland to the BR Research Division at Derby for structural analysis. The unfitted shell was used for body deformation tests and placed in the compression rig to simulate end loading pressures. It was eventually broken up at Derby. Before that, however, it is seen inside the Engineering Development Unit test hall.* **Author**

cope with passenger demand on the route and was put on display at the Ulster Folk and Transport Museum at Cultra Manor.

In March 2001 LEV3, or RB003 as it was more usually known, was moved by its owners, Northern Ireland Railways/ Translink, to the Downpatrick & County Down Railway Museum where it was returned to use and is still operational.

Two further four-wheel railbus vehicles were built under the joint BREL-Leyland initiative in 1984, both with a Class 141-style cab end.

The first vehicle, identified by BRE as RB002 and later to become BREL75 was basically a single-vehicle Class 141, but only with a single double-leaf door on each side, located at the vehicle end. This vehicle was designed for right-hand-drive use and was exported to Canada soon after assembly for trial running in both winter and summer conditions on the line between Thompson and Pikwitonei, Manitoba. It was returned to the UK in 1992 and was subsequently dumped at Derby Litchurch Lane Works, where it was used as office accommodation for the Total Quality Management team. It was eventually sold in 1999 to the Riverstown Railway in Dundalk, Ireland where it can be found today in non-operational condition.

The other Class 141 style railbus was identified as RB004 or 'The USA'. This was constructed at Derby from parts supplied from Workington and built as a demonstrator; it was shipped to the USA in 1984 and operated in a number of areas before being returned to the UK in 1996. For its use in the US, standard US-style knuckle couplers were fitted, as was a front end-mounted bell.

This vehicle was very different from the other prototypes in having driving controls on the right side of the cab end, with three sets of folding doors on one side and one on

Left: *The Federal Railroad Administration (FRA) of the USA ordered its own LEV, known as LEV2. This vehicle was assembled by D. Wickham of Ware, Hertfordshire. After assembly and prior to export it operated for a short time on the BR test track at Old Dalby. In the US it went into trial service on the Boston & Maine Railroad in 1980, and operated between Concord, New Hampshire and Lowell, Massachusetts. It is shown left at Old Dalby.* **Author**

Above: *On 25 April 1982 Railbus No 977020 operated under its own power from Bristol St Philips Marsh to Plymouth Laira depot to take part in an Open Day event. After the Open Day No 977020 is seen in the depot yard awaiting a path back to Bristol.* **Author**

the other. Front end-obstacle deflector plates were fitted and side steps provided for entry from track height. To conform with US rules and regulations extra headlights were fitted in the 'bumper' on both ends, together with wing mirrors. Air conditioning was also installed, mounted in a roof pod.

On return to the UK the vehicle was sent to Derby Litchurch Lane and stored. No further work could be found for the vehicle as a railbus, but by then the BRE-Transmark marketing of such vehicles to overseas countries was all but over. By 1997 the body, still mounted on railway wheels, was in use as an office at the works site.

While inside it was used as an office, the

Above Right: *In immaculate ex-production condition No 977020 stands in the yard at BREL Derby Litchurch Lane on 12 September 1981. In the background are a number of Mk3 sleeper body shells awaiting fitting out.* **Author**

Right: *To allow proving of the Railbus principle, No 977020 was placed into passenger service on the Bristol - Severn Beach branch from October 1981. It operated 'when available' for some eight months before returning to Derby. On 10 November 1981 the vehicle departs from Redland forming the 10.08 Bristol Temple Meads to Severn Beach.* **Author**

exterior was used for various paint trials and just before its eventual sale it was painted in dark blue with yellow and red squares.

After the vehicle was put up for sale, it was sold to the Embsay and Bolton Abbey Steam Railway in the Yorkshire Dales. In 2004 it was offered for sale and purchased by a group from the Telford Steam Railway who restored it to fully operational condition and painted it in mock 'Skipper' brown and cream livery as applied to the Western Region-allocated Class 142s.

Each of the prototype Railbus vehicles was powered by a single six-cylinder 200hp type TL11 underslung engine. ●

Above: *After finishing trials in mid-1982, LEV3 was sold to Northern Ireland Railways, where it was re-gauged to 5ft 3in and used on the Coleraine to Portrush line for around eight years. In 1990 the vehicle was taken out of service as its size could not cope with passenger demand and it was displayed at the Ulster Folk and Transport Museum at Cultra Manor. In March 2001 RB003, as it was usually known, moved to the Downpatrick & County Down Railway Museum where it is still is use. This view was taken on 17 February 2007 at Downpatrick.* **M. Collins**

Below: *BREL75, which was designed for right-hand driving, was exported to Canada soon after assembly for trial running in both winter and summer conditions on the line between Thompson and Pikwitonei, Manitoba. Complete with VIA bodyside branding, BREL75 is seen at Thompson, Manitoba on 30 May 1986. Note the bodyside running lights and North American style warning horns.* **David Othern**

Second Generation DMUs

Right: *After BREL75 was returned to the UK in 1992 it was dumped at BREL Derby Litchurch Lane Works, where it was used as office accommodation for the Total Quality Management team; firstly on wheels mounted on track and later dumped on the ground. Eventually it was sold in 1999 to the Riverstown Railway in Dundalk, Ireland where it can be found today as a non-operational exhibit and sadly, when seen in 2007, with some body damage. In this view the vehicle is seen at BREL Derby.* **Author**

Right: *Due to its historic importance as part of the development of passenger transport in the UK, RDB975874 or LEV1 was claimed by the National Railway Museum after final withdrawal from the Research & Development Division at Derby. The vehicle was transferred to the York site, firstly dumped in the museum's north yard before being stored in the annexe area. After a long time an agreement was reached and the vehicle was transferred to the North Norfolk Railway at Weybourne, where it was returned to an operational condition. It is viewed in the depot yard at Weybourne on 10 November 2007.*
Brian Morrison

Leyland Bus Mk 1 Coach Project

As part of the British Railways Board's quest to develop 'alternative transport vehicles' and following on from the perceived success of the Railbus concept, a locomotive-hauled variant was ordered. Leyland provided a 69ft long National bus-derived body structure which was mounted on the underframe of withdrawn Mk1 21234. The coach was assembled at the EDU in Derby and operated as RDB977091 on a limited passenger use on CrossCountry and West Coast services. Internally the vehicle has standard seats rather than bus seats, but lacked sound proofing and when in traffic resembled travelling in a tin can!

Right: *The vehicle is seen at Manchester while in use on the Brighton-Manchester corridor. It is now preserved on the East Kent Railway.*
Author

As discussed in the previous chapter, during the mid-1970s BR's Research and Development Division in Derby was investigating the possibility of transferring automotive (bus) technology to railways, and produced the Leyland Experimental Vehicle (LEV) in collaboration with Leyland Vehicles.

The LEV rode satisfactorily at speeds of up to 80mph during preliminary tests, and the test results were sufficiently promising for a two-car unit based on the design to be ordered for service trains. This became Class 140 and was a further marriage of Leyland National bus body sections with a railway underframe.

The Class 140 project rode alongside the Class 210 heavyweight DMU project with the contemporary plan to use the two types as a replacement for the entire aging DMMU fleet.

In respect of the Class 140 the underframe was manufactured by British Rail Engineering Limited, the body sections were fabricated at Leyland Workington and the vehicles were fully assembled at BREL Derby Litchurch Lane Works.

The Leyland National bus shells were produced in a highly mechanised purpose-built plant at Workington. The body was made up of modules 1,421mm long, which could be joined together to form a vehicle body of any length, although the width was fixed at 2,500mm (8ft 2½in) compared to the normal BR train width of 2,816mm (9ft 3in). All the body sections were riveted together using precision jigs, and no welding was used in assembly.

The high degree of accuracy in assembling the vehicle bodyshells enabled interior finishing panels and floors to be supplied to the factory pre-cut to size.

The body finishing panels were secured by means of moulded nylon clips without the use of tools, and all internal wiring looms were of the 'plug and socket' type. The result was that no skilled trades needed to be employed in the body production/assembly line.

The business specification for the body shell contained requirements which were to have a considerable influence on the adaptation of the

bus body to meet the needs of British Rail: -

* A seating capacity for the two-car unit of 102.
* The elimination of the step well in the doorway.
* Provision of a level floor.
* Provision of a gangway between the two vehicles.

In addition the structure was required to meet minimum end loadings without permanent deformation: - 150 tonnes compressive at the couplers, 40 tonnes compressive at the base or the bodyend pillars and 30 tonnes compressive at waist height of the body end and at cantrail height on the body end. These requirements were standard to all current designs or multiple units. The loads could have been reduced for the Class 140, but it was the request of the Inspecting Officer of Railways that they should apply to lightweight vehicles as well as those of traditional design.

The previous Leyland National design of front end with a large curved windscreen was unsuitable to meet end loads, particularly those above floor level. However, the length of the unit (15,998 cm - 52ft 6in) and the different

Below: *Some ten months before the Class 140 was seen in the yard at BREL Derby Litchurch Lane, the BRB press office released this artist's impression of the train, clearly showing the passenger door configuration, window positioning and the basic end style. From the release of this image and details on the train's interior, the controversy started.* **Author's collection**

Above: *The two bodyshell fabrications, formed of bus part sections were assembled at the Leyland bus factory in Workington and then shipped to BREL Derby for fitting onto a four-wheel chassis. Unlike the later production vehicles the Class 140 has a load bearing frame structure more in keeping with a traditional train design. The first bodyshell is seen nearing completion. The join between bus and rail vehicle is clearly visible just ahead of the cab side window.* **Author's collection**

load paths, due to the vehicle suspension and the weight of the various items of equipment under the vehicle, required a substantial underframe to support the bus body. This underframe extended to the ends of the vehicle, and provided for the compressive loading at the coupler. It also provided a good attachment for the collision pillars needed to meet the other end load conditions. The removal of the step well in the bus body led to a redesign of the doorway and the opportunity was taken to install an extra cantrail section, threaded through and

Right: *After the marriage of the bodyshells and chassis members at BREL, the Class 140 was transferred to the Engineering Development Unit and the RTC Derby for extensive static tests. No 140001 is seen inside the main test hall on 2 April 1982 while modification and upgrade work was being carried out prior to the next tranche of test and passenger runs being authorised.* **Author**

Left Top: *Some of the earliest main-line test running of the Class 140 was in February 1981 when the set, under the control of the BR Research Division, performed trial running over the Derby-Loughborough-Leicester route. On 26 April 1981 the set is seen at Loughborough.* **John Tuffs**

Left Below: *Although the Class 140 was very much a passenger-carrying train, it was always made available for the development engineers at Derby if needed. On 21 May 1982 the set is captured passing Clay Mills, Burton-on-Trent, returning to Derby after performing main line brake tests in the Birmingham area.* **John Tuffs**

The two-car unit had a small toilet compartment in one vehicle.

The underfloor-mounted engine provided on both vehicles was a Leyland TL80 6cyl horizontal turbocharged unit providing 218hp at 2100rpm. The drive to one axle of the vehicle is taken via a four-speed gearbox. The gearbox incorporated the free-wheel and reversing gear. Control of engine and gearbox is by means of conventional relays and electro-pneumatic valves.

Another aid to improved reliability was the provision of a double battery system on each vehicle, where one battery was concerned solely with engine starting. The battery was of 18 alkaline cells, and paired with the battery for lighting and control which had 19 alkaline cells, ensuring that the engine starter battery was charged. Charging was by two engine mounted alternators which had a total output of 120 amps at 30V, of which approximately half was available at engine idling speed.

Another aid to reliability was a device to shut down the engine after 10 minutes idling if the vehicle was stationary.

As part of fire prevention as far as possible horizontal surfaces which could accumulate debris that could become soaked in oil were eliminated, and no inflammable materials or lagging are used below the floor.

The two-axle suspension, designated AXI Pa, is derived from the design developed for the High Speed Freight Vehicle (another BR Research project), and was capable of an acceptable ride at speeds of up to 80mph. The axlebox was a yoke-shaped casting providing seats for the coil springs on either side of the axle; the upper ends of these springs engaged with retaining spigots on the subframe. Vertical and lateral control was by means of hydraulic dampers mounted between the axlebox and the subframe, with the coil springs contributing the necessary degree of lateral stiffness.

The wheelset was controlled longitudinally by means of traction rods between the axlebox and a bracket mounted on the subframe, the required stiffness being obtained from an assembly or rubber springs at the attachment or the bracket.

The brake assembly, using composition brakeblocks acting on the wheel tread, was also mounted on the axlebox because the high degree of lateral freedom of the suspension

attached to the bus roof structure to provide some much-needed longitudinal stability to the body.

The design of the driving cab was similar to the Class 210, including the use of high-impact windscreens, and this gave a desirable degree of standardisation.

A major departure from the standard bus body was in the design of the doors. The original bus doors, which cannot readily be locked, were replaced by a 'switch plug' type of door which has the door leaves mounted on vertical pillars which rotate to open or close. The mechanism was simple and robust; the doors open to the outside, needing no door pocket inside the vehicle, and the closing action gave a 'nip' on the door seals good enough to eliminate draughts.

The unit had a roof-mounted saloon heater similar to that used on the Leyland National bus, and fed with waste heat from the engine cooling system. Because the interior space of the Class 140 was greater than that of a bus, the system was supplemented by convector heaters, fed from engine cooling water.

In a rail operation, when the engine spends a considerable time idling, providing a low heat output, it was found necessary to equip the vehicle with an oil-burning water heater to boost the heat output if required. This arrangement also gave a degree of engine pre-heat and eased starting problems in cold weather. The driver's cab had its own heater.

A further departure from the Leyland National bus was in the seating. Standard BR outer-suburban seats were fitted.

Second Generation DMUs

Right: *After performing its initial trial passenger runs, the 140 undertook further testing at Derby before working for a lengthy period from Laira depot in Plymouth on Cornish branch line services. A slight modification to the livery was carried out by Plymouth staff when the 140001 running number was removed and replaced by the digits '140' on the front above the central gangway door, as shown in this illustration of the set at Plymouth on 14 April 1984.* **Author**

Below: *After the Class 140 was withdrawn from passenger service in Cornwall it initially returned to Derby and then Leeds where it was stored in the yard at Leeds Holbeck, being finally withdrawn from stock in 1990. Thankfully the set was saved for preservation and is currently on the Keith & Dufftown Railway. No 140001 is seen at Holbeck on 24 April 1989.* **Author**

would otherwise make correct alignment between block and wheel tread impossible.

The brake cylinder / slack adjuster assembly was flexibly mounted on the subframe and the pull rod was long enough to ensure that normal misalignments were accommodated without damage. A spring-actuated parking brake was fitted in the brake cylinder, so that when the vehicle was parked the brake would be applied as the air in the brake cylinder leaked off. The service brake was controlled by the Westcode System.

The floor height of the vehicles was 1,215mm above rail - slightly higher than the 'heritage' DMMU design at 1,157mm, this was due to the need to accommodate the power units and underslung equipment.

Testing of No 140001, composed of vehicles 55500 and 55501, commenced in early 1981

from the RTC Derby, which took the set on the Matlock line, the route to Crewe and the Midland Main Line to London Cricklewood.

The train was officially launched to the media at an event in Leeds on 4 June 1981, after which the train received BR blue and grey livery for display to the Directors General of the seven Passenger Transport Executives and commenced a national tour showing the proposed next generation of power; this included Newcastle on 22 June 1981, Carlisle on 24 June, Chester on 26 June, Cardiff on 29 June, Carmarthen on 30 June, Bristol on 1 July, Plymouth on 3 July, Derby on 6 July and Cambridge on 8 July.

After these displays, and intermingled with further testing, the set entered passenger service for four weeks from 13 July on the North Warwick line between Birmingham

and Stratford, followed by four weeks from 10 August in the Strathclyde area and four weeks from 7 September on the Preston to Colne route. From 5 October 1981 the set entered service (as available) on the Leeds - Barnsley and Sheffield route. Demonstration and display also took the unit on the Central Wales Line towards the end of 1981.

Development work on the 140 project came to an end in 1982 with follow-on orders for production Class 141 and 142 fleets placed. The Class 140 soldiered on for several years, working mainly in Cornwall, allocated to Laira; it was last recorded in passenger service in 1985, after which it was stored and transferred to Leeds Holbeck, where it remained for several years. The historic power twin is now preserved on the Keith & Dufftown Railway in Scotland. ●

3 Class 141

The Class 140 railbus with its added requirements took it away from the initial 'pure' bus-rail lightweight design and was not how the project was originally conceived. The additions of a 'standard' driving cab layout, body-strengthening, power doors, standard BR seats, and a toilet were not in the original criteria.

Therefore when the first squadron order for railbus stock was placed, classified 141 and numbered 141001-141020, many of these modifications were dropped. The Class 141 design did, however, retain a toilet and was designed and produced as a two-car unit, rather than a bus on rail wheels, but with very much a bus-type interior. Also, it was found that the end-loading requirements did not require such heavy re-engineering of the bus body as originally thought. The Department of Transport therefore authorised production of 20 Class 141 two-car units; it was agreed not to build a prototype, due to the amount of

experience already gained with LEVs and the Class 140s. Funding for the Class 141s was provided by West Yorkshire Passenger Transport Executive.

For the '141' fleet the Leyland National body was again built at Workington to a similar design as the Class 140. The body modules were built into a chassis, with the assemblies riveted together using precision jigs. The entire body module for each vehicle was then transferred to BREL's Derby Litchurch Lane Works, where it was fitted to the rail underframe.

As previously mentioned the standard Leyland National bus front was not able to meet all safety criteria, and a new design was derived, resulting in quite an attractive style of cab end, without the end doors for train crew access and emergency use that spoiled the appearance of the Class 140. The rail underframe which extends to the ends of the vehicle was designed to support all underfloor

equipment, including the diesel engine and gearbox.

In the body structure, the standard Leyland National stepwells were included by the mid-vehicle length passenger access doors on both sides, originally the doors were of the double folding Deans Type used on the Leyland National 2 buses, but these were subsequently changed. Hinged crew access doors were provided either side of the body immediately behind the cab. The design of the cab was such that the driver's door could be locked back into the bulkhead to provide a full width area separating the crew from the passenger compartment. Heating for the Class 141 was the same as that provided for the Class 140.

Unlike the Class 140, the Class 141 used Leyland National standard bus seating and trim, the passenger seats had moquette covers and a modified squab/cushion fixing to ease removal for cleaning or repair. Each two-car unit had one toilet compartment, housing a

Below: *The bus section body-shells for the first production railbus two-car set No 141001 take shape in the main erecting shop at Workington in March 1983. The main Leyland National 2 body sections cover the passenger area, while the section in advance of the first passenger window, the cab doorway and driving cab area are bespoke design using bus sections specially formed. The rather pleasing cab end was also specially designed to provide good visibility conforming to railway safety needs while still using sub-assembly techniques. The body sections are finished in a dark blue, slightly different from BR blue and more in line with another of Leyland's customers, Barrow Corporation.* **Author's collection**

toilet pan, wash basin, vanity unit and mirror. The water tank was located in the roof.

The train's main power equipment consisted of an underfloor-mounted engine on each vehicle of the Leyland TL 11 6cyl horizontal type, set to deliver 200hp at 1,950rpm. Each engine drove one axle of the vehicle and was transmitted via the four-speed gearbox, virtually identical to the Class 141 design.

The two-axle suspension system adopted was derived from the design developed for the high speed freight vehicle and the Advanced Passenger Train (APT-E) in its earliest form, and was capable of an acceptable ride at speeds of up to 80mph.

The 20 Class 141s entered service in Yorkshire between October 1983 and October 1984. Originally they were painted in a version of blue/grey, this quickly giving way to the WYPTE house colours of Verona green and buttermilk. Sadly the fleet's performance was poor, passengers and staff did not like them and the ride on Yorkshire track was inferior to that of the trains they replaced. The main complaint about the Class 141s was the cramped passenger accommodation which was within a standard bus width. The mechanical components were also troublesome in service, and even on the press demonstration run from Leeds, on which the editor travelled, performance was poor and adverse comments were made by all about the design.

The main technical problems involved the cable-operated air brake system which induced 'brake shudder' especially when cast iron brake blocks were used. This was reduced when composite brake blocks were fitted but this caused its own problems with interference to signalling reducing the train's presence on track circuit systems. Electrical problems were also prevalent, especially with the use of automotive systems involving a lot of small relays; in some cases these induced serious mechanical problems by giving wrong instructions to the gearbox.

It was soon after this that the mooted 'alternative' of building a new fleet of 'classic' bogie DMUs really began to surface, and the

Right: *The first production Class 141, No 141001, stands in the yard at BREL Derby Litchurch Lane in September 1983. At this time the set was painted in blue and grey livery, offset by a standard yellow warning end and a joint BR/West Yorkshire PTE MetroTrain logo on the bodyside.* **Author**

Below: *Soon after introduction problems became apparent with numerous services 'lost' due to technical problems; this was compounded by complaints by passengers and staff who disliked the cramped interiors of the new trains. Seen painted in West Yorkshire PTE green and buttermilk livery, set No 141020 with car No 55541 nearest the camera is seen in the bay at York on 8 November 1984 forming an evening service to Harrogate.* **Author**

Class 141 was thus destined to remain a 'one-off' fleet of just 20 units, in some respects (including the two-pipe air brake system) the trains were highly non-standard, and thus incompatible with the new-generation fleets. An idea which was canvassed as early as 1986 was to withdraw the entire fleet from BR service, refurbish them, and sell them to an overseas operator - replacing them with later designs of train such as the Classes 142, 143, 150. However, instead it was decided to refurbish and modify the '141s' to bring them up to scratch and make them compatible with Classes 150, 142, 143 and 144 which by then were being introduced and fitted with the EP (electro-pneumatic) brake; they also used BSI couplers which included physical, electrical and pneumatic connections.

By 1988 the Class 141s were withdrawn from service and taken to Hunslet-Barclay

at Kilmarnock for major upgrading; this involved replacement of much equipment including the entire brake system, plus fitting of a standard air/EP system, replacement of the original Tightlock couplers with automatic BSI units which included physical, pneumatic and electrical connections, removal of the nose-end multiple-control jumpers and cables, modifications to doors and upgrading of the gearbox.

The refurbished sets (which returned to traffic between June 1988 and August 1989 painted in standard WYPTE red and cream livery, were a little more reliable and reclassified as Class 141/1, numbered 141101-120 (not in the original order) and remained operational from Leeds Neville Hill until 1997 when they were replaced by Class 142s displaced by the introduction of newer stock on other lines.

One of the biggest problems with the Class 141s was their bus-width bodies which did not allow much passenger circulating space inside the vehicles - all subsequent designs were built to 'standard' railway width.

As the sets had many more years of work left in their equipment, the original plan to sell the sets for overseas use was now adopted; when withdrawn in 1997 the units were stored and offered for sale. Set No 141118 entered a short period of service with Serco at Derby as a weed-control vehicle known as 'Flower', while others were stored and taken over by Cotswold Rail.

Thirteen sets (141101/102/105/107/109/ 111/114-120, including the set used by Serco) were later sold to The Islamic Republic of Iran Railways (eight remain in passenger service), while four are preserved in the UK (141103/108/110/113), two were exported to Holland (141106/112) and one, No 141104, was broken up at Neville Hill in September 1993 following collision damage. ●

Left: *Allocated to Leeds Neville Hill, the Class 141s could be found operating on most West Yorkshire local routes as well as working through to technically South Yorkshire stations in Doncaster and Sheffield. In a far cry from today's scene at Leeds City, where electric power reigns supreme in the bay platforms, this view taken on 12 February 1987 shows the 'Heritage' and 'Pacer' era. Set No 141013 and 141011 wait to depart with afternoon services to Knaresborough and Skipton, while a 'Heritage' Class 101 DMMU stands the other side of the platform face.* **Author**

Left: *The interior of the Class 141s, as with all the 14x DMUs, was rather spartan when first introduced. This is a view taken from the cab end looking down the saloon to the lockable bench seat area, which could be converted into a luggage or mail section. The seats are of a different design on either side; those on the left can be folded down to provide a flat stowage surface, while those on the right are of the fixed type.* **Author**

Second Generation DMUs

Above: *On a bright 13 March 1989, refurbished set No 141103 passes Healey Mills forming the 14.17 Wakefield to Huddersfield service. The ride in this area with a sizeable amount of point work was described by one regular passenger on the route as 'lively'.* **Author**

Right: *By the mid-1990s most Class 141s had been taken out of service and after original storage by owners Porterbrook Leasing at Leeds Neville Hill were taken to RFS Engineering at Doncaster for long-term store pending sale or disposal. Three sets with No 141103 nearest the camera stand in the works yard on 5 March 1996. Set No 103 was later sold into preservation and is presently on the Weardale Railway in a fully operational condition.* **Author**

Right: *Literally parked in the middle of a field, withdrawn set No 141116 was for several years parked in the rail yard at the fire and accident training compound at Morton-in Marsh. At this location sections of motorway, industrial and residential housing and rail tracks are set up for training of the emergency services. In the background a section of a fictitious motorway can be seen with damaged vehicles, while the '141' sits among the grass. This set, through Cotswold Rail, was later one of the group exported to Iran. Photographed on 20 July 2000.* **Author**

Second Generation DMUs

Although a complete re-think of the future needs of suburban, rural and branch line travel was made in the early to mid-1980s, which tended to favour the more traditional designs, great desire still existed to further develop the 'railbus' concept. The Leyland Bus/BREL partnership set out to design a standard-width rail vehicle body for the 'railbus' project, answering many of the major critics of the Class 140 and 141 products. By mid-1983 this was accepted by the British Railways Board in principle and detailed specifications were agreed, culminating in an order (the first true production order for a railbus train) being placed on 16 January 1984 for 50 twin-vehicle sets.

The redesign to a standard rail-width vehicle enabled 3+2 seating to be installed, increasing the passenger load of a single set to a maximum of 120. The changes also allowed a more pleasing front-end design to be styled, while still retaining the modular bus design.

The body sections for the order were fabricated at Leyland Bus, Workington and transported by road to BREL Derby Litchurch Lane for fitting onto a BREL-built underframe assembly. These too were assembled in a modular style, allowing the bus body sections to be lowered onto mounting pivots and secured to the chassis by bolts. Pneumatic and electrical connections were made by plus joints meaning assembly was fast and accurate.

The first set, No 142001 of a range numbering from 142001-050, was tested over the Midland Main Line route to Leicester, Kettering, Bedford and Cricklewood from June 1985. The first 14 sets off the production line were destined for use in Manchester, funded by the Manchester PTE and were painted in orange and brown livery, complemented with full yellow warning ends and joint Manchester PTE and BR bodyside logos. During the course of production the sets became known as 'Pacer', a name which has stuck ever since and become applied to all of the 14x designs.

The second tranche of sets to emerge from Derby were perhaps the most controversial. Destined for use on Devon and Cornish branch lines and allocated to Laira in Plymouth, units 142015-027 were specially finished in traditional brown and cream livery and locally renamed as 'Skipper' sets. These 13 sets were soon heavily criticised by staff, passengers and user groups, with complaints over seating and interior comforts but, above all, about rough riding and the extreme noise of wheel squeal on the curvaceous tracks of Devon/Cornwall branch lines. The squealing caused by the dry interface between wheel flange and rail web was also found to seriously damage both rails and wheels, with countless sets out of traffic for lengthy periods and in some areas replacement of rails was necessary. Other serious problems surrounded failures of the self-changing gear transmissions.

The West Country problems resulted in the sets' transfer to the Leeds and Newcastle areas from mid-1987, being replaced by 'heritage' sets returned to service.

Sets built from No 142028 were allocated to the Manchester area and the North East, being painted in the Provincial business colour of two-tone blue and white.

While the first 50 sets were being delivered, a follow-on order was placed on 7 October 1985 for an additional 46 units, these were delivered in 1986-87.

Major operating problems befell the Class 142 fleet in all areas and a major refurbishment plan was put together by the late 1990s, with Hunslet Barclay of Kilmarnock being awarded the upgrade work.

Originally the Class 142s were fitted with one Leyland TL11 engine of 205hp under each vehicle; this drove the road wheels by way of a mechanical self-changing gearbox. The engine and particularly the transmission gave problems; both were replaced on upgrading. The new engine was a Cummins LTA10-R of 230hp, driving a Voith T211r hydraulic

Below: *Parked in the works yard at Derby Litchurch Lane on 30 September 1985, brand-new set No 142008 awaits final completion and inspection, prior to a 'hand-over' test run to Bedford and return before transfer to Newton Heath depot in Manchester. Note the original four-section doors and orange, brown and white 'Manchester' livery. When the author visited Derby Litchurch Lane Works on 30 September 1985 no fewer than 14 sets were under various stages of construction for Manchester and Devon/Cornwall-area use.* **Author**

transmission. Under the original design four section double-fold doors were fitted, which gave enormous trouble through unreliability and were replaced with a more rigid double-section folding door. The original cable-worked brake system, which was again unsatisfactory, was replaced by a conventional direct-acting air system. The main passenger saloons were left largely unaltered, but a modified fire detection system was fitted.

Following attention, the overall operating area of the 96 strong fleet enlarged, with a number of units transferring to the Liverpool and Merseyside PTE operating areas, emerging in Merseytravel yellow livery. Other sets were deployed in the Newcastle area, some branded in Tyne & Wear yellow livery, while the main stamping areas of the class around Leeds and Yorkshire remained.

As time progressed and more local control of the railways preceeded privatisation in the mid 1990s came several local initiatives at upgrading the fleet, several were equipped with new interiors using rail style 2+2 seating rather than bus style 2+3 configurations.

After privatisation the fleet were largely deployed by the Northern (originally Northern Spirit). First North Western, Arriva (Merseyrail) operators. Later with franchise changes and units becoming redundant, the allocation split in 2008 is 66 sets working for Northern, 15 for Arriva Trains Wales and 12 for First Great Western.

In one of the biggest ever turn-arounds in

Above: *The 14 orange Manchester PTE sets remained in their intended area for many years. Here on 27 March 1990 set No 142005 stops at Hapton while forming the 11.20 Blackpool South to Colne service.* **Author**

Below: *The pioneer of the fleet, No 142001, now operated by First Great Western, approaches Chinley on 20 July 1981 forming the 12.10 Manchester Piccadilly to Sheffield service.* **Author**

Above: *Once the Class 142 railbus body shells were completed at Leyland Bus, Workington, they were transported by road to Derby Litchurch Lane for marrying up with a locally-built chassis assembly. Often a large number of vehicles were mounted on their chassis and then 'parked up' in the works yard to await fitting out and testing. On 30 September 1985, one orange vehicle for set 142012 and two brown and cream cars for sets 142017 and 142021 stand in the works yard in company with a Northern Ireland Railways Class 450 DMU vehicle awaiting fitting out after delivery from BREL York Works.* **Author**

stock allocations, FirstGroup took over 12 sets for deployment in Devon from the winter timetable change in 2007, replacing Class 150s, 153s and 158s from FGW-Local services. Massive controversy surrounded the return to West Country use, but the options were few; if a service was to be retained on some branchlines, the cheaper-to-operate 'Pacer' sets needed to be used.

There have always been some serious concerns about the body strength of the 14x designs in the case of an accident, which was amply illustrated when an empty four-car formation of Class 142 stock was struck at around 50mph by a Class 87-powered West Coast express at Winsford on 23 June 1999. The impact ripped the body structure off the underframe, and had the train been carrying passengers a number of people would have been seriously injured or killed. After this it was planned either to restrict the railbus vehicles to secondary routes or replace them, but in 2009 no such moves have materialised and the 14x fleets look set to remain in service on medium and long distance services for at least another 5-10 years. Internal upgrades have recently been made to many sets. ●

Below: *After allocation to Plymouth Laira for Devon and Cornish branch line use, the Class 142s, locally known as 'Skippers', soon fell from favour, with passenger and staff complaints about poor interior quality when viewed alongside the 'Heritage' stock they replaced, rough riding and noise. On 20 April 1987, set No 142026 departs from Newton Abbot and heads towards Aller Junction forming the 10.20 Exeter St Davids to Paignton service. In Devon the Class 142s were rostered to operate on the Exeter to Paignton, Barnstaple and Exmouth routes.* **Author**

Right: *After the first 27 sets had been built in Manchester orange and Devon and Cornwall brown and cream livery, the standard provincial colours of two-tone blue, off-set by a white stripe with full yellow warning ends was applied to the remainder of the build. Following deployment in Manchester and the West of England, the next area to see Class 142 or 'Pacer' activity was around Yorkshire, Humberside and Lincolnshire. Here the design was more welcome with fewer passenger complaints. However serious mechanical problems still prevailed which saw a high casualty rate, not meeting the minimum of performance targets. On 15 March 1989, set No 142074 of the 'follow-on' order passes Howden forming the 12.26 York to Hull service.* **Author**

Right: *Multiple compatibility existed between the Class 142s and Class 150s and pairings were not uncommon on the Manchester to York 'Trans Pennine' route. However, with the different braking systems used on the two designs some serious 'snatching' was reported by frequent passengers. Displaying its original provincial livery, set No 142077 and a Class 150/2 arrive at York on 14 May 1988 and approach York Holgate Junction.* **Ian Allan Library**

Right: *The keen interest by Transmark in selling the joint Leyland Bus/BREL 'railbus' design overseas continued further than just the prototype single vehicle railbus, with production Class 142 No 142049 being exported to Canada for demonstration and display at the World's Fair, held in Vancouver in August 1986. After display and with temporary extra headlights the set was used on trial and show runs in British Columbia. On 31 December 1986 the set was captured at Ville-St-Pierre in Montreal.* **Hughes W. Bonin via Don McQueen**

Above: *Under the sectorisation of British Railways in the years immediately prior to privatisation, the Class 142s were operated by the Regional Railways business. In addition to Regional Railways branding, a number of sponsored sets, funded by Passenger Transport Executives, were dressed in the house colours of these authorities. Sets funded by Merseytravel and used in the Liverpool area were painted in a rather attractive yellow and white scheme offset by a black and grey mid-height body band. Frequently these sets were recorded outside their intended operating area, as was the case when this view of set No 142054 was recorded at Doncaster on 25 June 1990 forming the 09.15 Doncaster to Manchester service.* **Author**

Left: *Units allocated to Heaton depot in Newcastle and funded by Tyne & Wear PTE were also outshopped in yellow livery, this time offset by a mid-blue bodyside band at waist height. In the days before the application of orange cantrail safety stripes, set No 142019, one of the original West Country brown and cream sets, departs from Hartlepool with a Newcastle Central to Middlesbrough working.* **Author**

Left: *Following privatisation in the mid-1990s a number of new liveries were introduced. Under the original 1997 scheme the Yorkshire, North East and Trans Pennine operation, including the S&C route, trains to Liverpool, Blackpool, Scarborough and Hull were taken over by MTL Trust Holdings, which traded as Northern Spirit, adopting a livery incorporating a large letter 'N' on the bodyside. MTL Holdings sold out to Arriva PLC in 2000. 'Pacer' No 142065 is seen at Leeds City on the day of the official livery launch, 21 May 1998, when a Class 142 was displayed in turquoise house colours and a Class 158 in maroon, depicting the local and main line colours and branding of the company. Some slight variations were subsequently made to this livery application.* **Author**

Second Generation DMUs

Right: *Class 142s repainted in the early 1990s emerged in Regional Railways colours, based on a grey and blue scheme, offset by a light blue and white bodyside stripe. Horizontal blue and white stripes were applied under the cabside windows. The early 1990s saw the fleet commence work in South Wales, and on 25 June 2002, set No 142090 arrives at Pontypridd with a service from Cardiff to Treherbert.* **Author**

Right: *Sporting the old First North Western blue and gold star livery, but with stick-on Northern branding, set No 142027 passes Seascale Golf Course on the Cumbrian Coast Line on 5 June 2007 while forming the 12.41 Carlisle to Lancaster via Barrow service. This livery scheme probably looks the most impressive on this short body.* **Nathan Williamson**

Below: *From December 2007, 12 Class 142s were taken from store and transferred to First Great Western at Exeter for use on the Exeter to Paignton, Barnstaple and Exmouth branch line services, replacing Class 150 and 153 sets. All 12 units were painted in the dark blue of former operator First North Western, and were thus cosmetically respectable and with First Great Western branding looked neat and tidy. However their reception in the west was somewhat hostile with passengers, passenger groups and staff all demanding the sets be taken out of service, as it was felt that the trains they replaced were in better condition and of better quality. However, in 2008 the sets were still in traffic, running reasonably well. On 29 December 2007, set No 142064 departs from Dawlish forming the 10.20 Exmouth to Paignton all stations service.* **Author**

5 Class 143

When the squadron fleets of railbus stock was authorised, the BRB decided to take the project down the avenue of multi-sourcing, with the orders being split among different builders.

Under the original railbus plan a batch of 25 two-car sets, given the classification 143, was funded for use in the Newcastle area. The tender order process saw the construction contract go to Walter Alexander for the bus bodies rather than Leyland, with the underframe chassis assembled by Hunslet-Barclay in their factory in Kilmarnock, Scotland. The official order for the build was sanctioned on 16 January 1984, with a 24-month delivery timescale.

This build again used the full rail body width and incorporated a slightly more pleasing body profile; the same basic configuration as used on the Class 142 was followed.

Traction power was provided by one Leyland TL11 engine under each vehicle with Self Changing Gears transmission.

Construction progressed well in Kilmarnock and the first complete two-car set, allocated the number 143001, was delivered to the RTC, Derby for commissioning in late summer 1985.

Testing over the main line as far south as Cricklewood was recorded in late September with an official press preview of the class between Derby and Matlock running on 18 October.

The sets were finished in the then Provincial business sector livery of two-tone blue and white, except the final six which were finished in Tyne and Wear Pacer livery.

The Class 143s, allocated to Heaton for Newcastle area operation soon became problematic; much like the Class 141s and 142s, difficulties mainly surrounded power units and gearboxes. As early as mid-1988 one set No 143003 was transferred to Doncaster Works for gearbox replacement using a Voith unit.

After receiving Class 142s in the Newcastle area some renumbering of the Class 143s was made with numbering in the 1436xx series being followed, except for the Tyne and Wear six which were numbered in the 1433xx series for a short period.

Redeployment of the Provincial sector assets took place in 1992-93 when progressively all sets were transferred to Cardiff Canton for use in the Cardiff and Bristol area.

Major refurbishment of the fleet commenced at Doncaster in 1993 when, much in line with similar work on Class 142s, new Cummins LTA10R engines of 230hp were fitted together with Voith T211r hydraulic transmissions; this work did improve performance.

After privatisation of the UK rail system in the mid-1990s, the Class 143 fleet was taken over by Porterbrook Leasing, with three sets officially owned by Rhondda Cynan Taff District Council and three sets by Rail Assets Investments.

The various changes of franchise since privatisation has now stabilised; in 2008, 16 sets were operated by Arriva Trains Wales for Cardiff area branch line use, and seven sets operate for First Great Western on Bristol suburban area services. One set, No 143615, was condemned following fire damage in October 2004 at Nailsea & Blackwell.

Originally the Class 143s were fitted with standard bus interiors using a 3+2 seating configuration; following refurbishment all sets now have a standard railway interior using the low-density 2+2 seating style, with accommodation for 106 passengers (reduced from 122 when introduced). ●

Below: *Painted in 'as-built' BR Provincial two-tone blue and white livery, the doyen of the class, No 143001, is seen at Matlock on 18 October 1985 during the 'lay-over' of the fleet's press demonstration run from Derby. A certain amount of freedom was given to the builders of each of the production railbus fleets, with Walter Alexander incorporating a two-section folding door and a more conventional location for the door release warning lights (adjacent to the door openings) rather than on the roof line as on the Class 142.* **John Tuffs**

Above: *The final six of the Heaton-allocated Class 143s were painted in yellow, white and blue Tyne & Wear Pacer livery and branded such on the lower body panel, together with a BR double-arrow logo. Set No 143024 is seen at Middlesbrough on 17 August 1987 forming a service to Nunthorpe, located on the single line to Battersby.* **Author**

Right: *In the period leading up to privatisation, the Class 143s were operated under the Regional Railways banner and transferred to South Wales at Cardiff Canton for use in the Cardiff and Bristol areas. While most maintenance work was carried out at Cardiff, heavy overhauls and refurbishment was undertaken at Doncaster Works. Seen on 2 May 1995, one vehicle from set No 143623 sits on works accommodation stands while a major component exchange maintenance exam is undertaken.* **Author**

Above: *Once allocated to Cardiff Canton for Cardiff area use alongside the Class 150/2 sets, the Class 143s settled down to provide a very reliable, but sometimes rather lively service, operating firstly for BR Regional Railways and from 1996 the private sector. On 6 April 1992, set No 143607 stands alongside Class 150/2 'Sprinter' No 150278 at Radyr forming the 14.46 all stations service to Coryton. The Class 150 is working the 14.02 Aberdare to Barry service.* **Author**

Left: *Carrying the rather attractive Valley Lines livery, set No 143610 approaches the station stop at Pontypridd on 25 June 2002 with a service bound for Barry Island. Several different operators and trading names have been found in the Welsh Valleys since privatisation in the area. On 13 October 1996, when Prism Rail were awarded the franchise, the title changed to Cardiff Valley Railway, Valley Lines and Wales & West, before the franchise was transferred to National Express group in 2000. In December 2003 the franchise again changed when Arriva Trains Wales took over operations.* **Author**

Left: *Upon privatisation, the Class 143s were allocated for use by both the Cardiff Valley and Wales & West operation; the sets operated by Wales and West were repainted in dark blue and on repainting sported pictogram liveries advertising travel in the Bristol area. On 25 June 2002, set No 143611 and Class 150/2 No 150276 make ready to depart from Newport with a Bristol Temple Meads to Cardiff service.* **Author**

Above: *The Class 143s seldom operated west of Exeter in regular service, but due to shortages of stock some workings on through services from Bristol to Exeter and Paignton were recorded. On 6 April 2002, Bristol blue-liveried set No 143613 was used by Exeter depot after being stabled overnight to form an Exeter to Exmouth service and then the 10.54 Exmouth to Paignton, seen traversing the Sea Wall at Parsons Tunnel, Teignmouth. Crewing the Class 142s in this area was always a problem with only limited numbers of train crew passed for their operation.* **Author**

Below: *Following the transfer of the Cardiff area franchise to Arriva Trains, the company house colours were soon applied by home depot Cardiff Canton. Looking rather attractive in turquoise and grey, set No 143609 approaches Cardiff with a service bound for Coryton on 5 November 2007. Note the new style of route display.* **Author**

6 Class 144

The final batch of railbus-derived multiple units to be ordered were classified as Class 144. Funded by West Yorkshire Passenger Transport Executive, an order for 23 two-car sets was placed on 7 October 1985, concurrent with the second order for Class 142s.

The Class 144s used the same Alexander bus bodies, but this time the chassis and running gear was provided by BREL Derby Litchurch Lane who also carried out the final assembly work. Production took place in 1986-87, deliveries to Leeds Neville Hill progressing between September 1986 and July 1987.

During the course of delivery extra WYPTE funding was found to enable 10 intermediate non-driving vehicles to be built, these became the only intermediate railbus vehicles ever built and were marshalled with the final 10 sets of the build, Nos 144014-023. However, due to the timescale of delivery of the intermediate vehicles, the sets were initially delivered as two-car sets and returned to Derby Works in March 1988 for the intermediate cars to be inserted.

In keeping with the earlier railbus designs, when originally delivered Leyland TL11 engines and Self Changing gearboxes were fitted, these being replaced in the early 1990s

during refurbishment with standard Cummins engines and Voith transmissions.

Sets were launched into traffic painted in a very distinctive deep maroon and buttermilk livery with full yellow warning ends and joint BR and West Yorkshire PTE (later Metro) branding. Under the BR Regional Railways passenger business sets were repainted in Regional Railways blue and grey colours.

Seating was provided in the standard bus style 2+3 layout and a toilet was located in one driving car.

These sets have always operated from Leeds Neville Hill on local duties, which on occasions has seen fleet members as far north as Carlisle on S&C duties.

Upon rail privatisation in the mid-1990s, the fleet passed to the control of Northern Spirit and later Arriva Trains Northern and now Northern Rail.

Major interior refurbishment in 2003-04 has seen significant improvements with interior comfort, 2+2 seats are now provided and the sets appear to have a better ride characteristic than other 'Pacer' types.

Following the early 2000s refurbishment a revised Metro livery was applied, still retaining the maroon red, but now offset by grey/silver half roundels on the bodysides. ●

Right: *Set No 144021, which was augmented to a three-car set in March 1988, is seen in multiple with set No 144009 on the outskirts of York on 16 May 1987 forming the 09.20 Leeds to Scarborough duty. Delivery and commissioning of the '144s' was rapid, with few on line faults and teething problems.* **Ian Allan Library**

Below Right: *The Class 144 'Pacer' build could be found operating to all corners of the WYPTE area, as well as many towns outside the main operating region, including Skegness, Carlisle, Manchester and even on the Esk Valley line between Middlebrough and Whitby. On 20 July 1989, set No 144003 stands at Marsden station with the 17.55 service from Selby.* **Author**

Below: *As soon as the joint BR/West Yorkshire PTE announcement was made that a fleet of new suburban and main-line diesel units were to be ordered, an artist's impression of both types was released to the railway media at a press conference held in Leeds. The painting of the Class 144 was very accurate, the only item missing being the destination indicator in the centre window. The inclusion of a joint WYPTE/BR logo on the front was not carried forward to the production train.* **Author's Collection**

Left: *One of the main routes on which the Class 144s can be seen is the York to Leeds and York to Hull lines, where their capacity of just 88 seated passengers is frequently insufficient for the patronage of the line. Set No 144002 departs south from York on 11 November 1994 forming a local service to Hull.* **Author**

Middle: *In the immediate period prior to privatisation a number of Class 142s were outshopped in BR Regional Railways blue and grey livery, offset by a white and light blue body band. This scheme made the sets virtually indistinguishable from the Class 143 sets. After privatisation the livery remained branded with the new operator's name, in this case Arriva. Set No 144012 is seen between duties at Sheffield on 28 August 2002.* **Author**

Bottom: *Sheffield station is a major hub of second-generation DMU activity with members of most classes recorded at one time or another. Looking down at the stations north end, three-car Class 144 No 144020 departs from Sheffield on 28 August 2002 forming the 10.15 service to Leeds via Wakefield.* **Author**

Above: *Sporting Northern elliptical livery of grey and WYPTE maroon and running alongside the Keadby & Stainforth Canal at Godnow Bridge near Crowle on 31 May 2006, No 144007 forms the 16.19 from Scunthorpe to Lincoln, via Sheffield.* **Brian Morrison**

Below: *The 10 three-car Class 144s tend to be used for the busiest services operating in the Leeds-York area, with the middle MS providing an extra 58 standard class seats when compared with a standard two-car set. Parked in the north facing bay at York on 8 April 2006, set No 144019 awaits departure to Leeds via Harrogate.* **Brian Garrett**

In the late 1970s considerable time was spent by the BRB on evaluation of replacement traction for the then aging DMMU fleet, a number of propositions were made, including the 'Railbus' concept previously detailed. However, for longer distance, cross-country or even short-haul InterCity services a more substantial train was needed, hence the evolution of the Class 210 DEMU project with above-floor-mounted engine.

To evaluate a number of proposals it was agreed to build two prototype trains of similar design, one with luggage space and first class accommodation for main line use and the other for more local operations.

At an early stage in planning it was agreed to introduce some form of standardisation for the proposed future fleet builds of the design, much in line with the BRB's policy of standardisation within the EMU builds such as the 313, 314, 315, 507 and 508 designs.

For the new generation of Class 210 DMU, it was agreed to standardise on the proposed Class 317 and 455 (then classified 510) EMUs, broadly based on Mk3 coach technology.

Design specifications for the Class 210 were complex and required compatibility with the new EMU classes (317) in terms of maximum speed, coupling arrangement, braking and control systems, enabling dual power trains to operate if needed. The new design also stipulated that crew governed, passenger operated sliding doors be installed, with an open passenger layout.

Gangways throughout the train were a requirement as were end corridor connections, meaning that the above floor engine mounted powercars needed a side gangway of at least 560mm for passengers to pass.

The design criteria for the two prototype trains called for a train suitable for short distance 6-25 mile commuter journeys as well as main line trips of between 100 and 125 miles. To try out and prove different designs the two prototypes were quite different. Set No 210001 was a four-car set formed driving motor brake second, trailer composite lavatory, trailer second and driving trailer second, while the three-car set No 210002 was formed driving motor second, trailer second and driving trailer second. On the four car set the driving motor standard incorporated a luggage compartment rendering only one third of the vehicle for passenger use (two bays), while on the three-car set the driving motor second had no luggage space and three seating bays. The total accommodation for the three-car set was 203 second class and the four-car 22 first and 232 second class. One-third-width driving cabs were provided on driving motor and driving trailer vehicles. Second class passenger seating was in the 2+3 style while the first class portion of the TC vehicle in set 210001 was in the low-density 2+2 style.

During an early stage in design, sliding plug passenger doors were considered, but by the time construction commenced, these were ruled out as more development work was required before squadron introduction could be considered.

Unlike previous designs of DMU, no guard's office was provided, and in keeping with modern EMU designs the guard used the rear driving cab non-driving side as his riding position.

The Class 210s were constructed by BREL at their Derby Litchurch Lane (driving cars) and York (intermediate cars) works and used many common features found on the Mk3 design, the structure was load bearing throughout. The power cars were a complex vehicle to produce and were a major adaptation of the Mk3 structure, requiring strengthening in the area of the power and cooler groups and changes to provide a roof opening.

The space for the power units and associated equipment was very limited with the requirement for a through passenger/staff walkway down one side, thus only a limited number of engine designs could be considered.

As the two sets were prototypes it was decided to equip each with a different engine.

Below: *While building of the driving cars and final assembly was carried out at BREL Derby Litchurch Lane, the three Class 210 intermediate vehicles were assembled on the coaching stock production line at York Works and then transported by rail within the consist of a freight train to Derby for marshalling up. On 2 April 1982, the three-car set No 210002 is seen under test in the works yard at Derby. As can be seen by this view from the driving trailer second end the design was identical to the Class 317.* **Author**

The four-car set was fitted with GEC supplied derivative of the Paxman Valenta designated as 6RP200L set to develop 1,125hp, while the three-car set carried a MTU 12V296 TC 12 engine of 1,140hp.

Control and electrical equipment was again dual sourced, with packages provided by Brush and GEC. Traction equipment consisted of four axle-hung traction motors on the power car. Underslung fuel tanks and battery boxes were also provided on this vehicle. Standard convection heating was fitted throughout.

Once assembled at Derby Litchurch lane and static testing was complete the two sets passed to the Engineering Development Unit at the

RTC for trials and dynamic tests. These were carried out firstly over the London Midland main line to Bedford and Cricklewood before more adventurous testing to various locations around the UK took place, this included periods of passenger use in Scotland and the North West.

Eventually the sets were transferred to Reading depot and deployed on the Western Region suburban routes from Paddington to Reading, Oxford and Bedwyn, where their performance was excellent. Maintenance was carried out at Reading depot and the sets remained in passenger use until 1987 when both were returned to the RTC Derby.

By now the over-specified Class 210 project was all but over, with the 15X designs being accepted as standard for the future of the non-main line railway.

Several of the former Class 210 vehicles saw further use. TC No 58000 (later 60450) was rebuilt by the EDU, Derby into No RDB977645 for development work on the all-electric vehicle project, while cars 57001 (60401), 54000 (60300) and 54001 (60301) were used as a traction development unit for AC traction and numbered 316999 and DC traction as 457001. Car 57000 (60400) was eventually rebuilt to EMU standards as car 67400 for use in Class 455 No 455920. ●

Right and Below: *Once on the Western Region for normal passenger deployment, the sets were allocated to Reading, where a limited number of drivers and guards were trained in their operation. Being a total change from their previous charges, the two sets were well liked by train crews and passengers, offering improved working and travelling conditions. The driving cab was more in keeping with an EMU, and was laid out with left hand controlled three position brake valve and a power controller operated by the right hand. Of course, having a diesel-electric transmission no messy gear changing was required. Set No 210002, the three-car set powered by the 12 cylinder MTU 12V396 TC 12 engine is seen at Paddington from both ends on 1 November 1984 awaiting departure with the 15.04 all-stations service to Reading.*
Both: **Author**

Left: *In normal operation on the Western Region, the two Class 210 units would work with their power car at the west end, which provided the most effective maintenance position at Reading depot. On 12 August 1983, the three-car set No 210002 departs from the then staggered up platform at West Ealing forming the 12.30 Slough to London Paddington stopping service.* **Author**

Below: *In the days before overhead power lines were erected in the London area of the Great Western main line, photography was much easier, with some excellent views of the mass of diesel locomotives and multiple-unit operations in the Acton area visible from several overbridges in the area. Viewed at the west end of Acton yard and overlooking the London Underground connection which terminates at Ealing Broadway and the LUL overbridge of the Piccadilly Line, four-car set No 210001 traverses the up slow line on 28 April 1984 forming the 09.52 Reading to Paddington semi-fast service. A London Underground Central Line train is seen on the right forming a service to Epping.* **Author**

Second Generation DMUs

Above: *Led by the luggage van-fitted power car No 53001, set No 210001, powered by the Paxman 6RP200L engine developing 1,125hp passes Ruscombe travelling over the down local track on 14 June 1985 forming the 11.01 Paddington to Oxford semi-fast service. The set's first class accommodation is provided in the centre of the intermediate vehicle coupled to the DTS at the far end. By the time this view was taken an 'L' prefix to the running number had been applied.* **Author**

Right: *The old and new order of DMU traction pass at West Ealing on 12 August 1983. Three-car set No 210002 departs from West Ealing station forming the 13.15 Paddington to Slough, while Class 117 Pressed Steel three-car set No L416 heads towards London Paddington with a stopping service from Reading.* **Author**

Right: *Considerable life was left in the Class 210 vehicles after they completed their test and evaluation period. All seven cars were returned to the RTC Derby where several found further use. Three vehicles 57001 (60401), 54000 (60300) and 54001 (60301) were rebuilt for AC traction development for Network SouthEast and formed with a Class 313 vehicle as a four-car train. Numbered 316999, the set was used on the Great Eastern AC network based at Clacton, where this view of the set was taken on 5 April 1990.* **Author**

8 Class 150

The real story of the Second Generation DMU starts with the contract for two prototype three-car sets placed with British Rail Engineering Ltd (BREL) in March 1983 - a similar contract was also placed with Metro-Cammell (See Class 151 section).

The BR DM&EE/BREL design, based on the Mk 3 coach, became the Class 150. Aided by the fact that BREL's York works was already tooled for Mk 3 EMU production, BREL completed the first Class 150 three months ahead of schedule, being handed over to the BR Provincial Sector on 8 June 1984.

The two '150' prototypes each consisted of three vehicles, gangwayed only within the set, allowing smartening-up of the front end design compared to the Class 210; however, as time proved, by the time the largest batch of the production Class 150 order was placed, gangway doors were returned.

The two original Class 150s were very much development trains, fitted with a different power equipment package for evaluation. All vehicles were powered, and driving cabs fitted to the outer end of each three-car set. Up to four units could operate in multiple. Maximum design speed was 75mph (120km/h).

Body construction incorporated a steel skin, rails and pillars welded together. The roof section was corrugated mild steel. The body structure could withstand 150 tonnes at coupler level and meet all UIC end-load requirements. The vehicle was designed for a 30-year fatigue life.

Sound insulation was important in design, and the use of an anti-drumming compound applied as a spray within the body structure improved interior noise, this was supplemented by fibreglass thermal and acoustic insulation in the bodyside, floor and roof. Bogie design reduced the level of track sound.

The first unit built, No 150001, was powered by a Cummins NT-855-R5 engine rated at 285hp, driving a Voith 211 hydraulic transmission, Gmeinder final drive assemblies were provided (this later became the standard traction package). The second

unit No 150002 was fitted with Rolls-Royce Eagle C6 280 HR engines rated at 280hp. This drove a Self Changing Gears R500 automatic gearbox via a carden shaft. The final drive assemblies were supplied by SCG.

The bogies used were a development of the successful BT13 family. Secondary suspension was by air-bags, and incorporated a levelling valve for maintaining standard floor height. Air operated tread brakes using composition blocks were filled.

Fully automatic BSI couplers were fitted instead of Tightlock couplers at the outer ends, enabling units to be coupled and uncoupled without the need for shunting. Within each set the cars were coupled by semi-permanent bar couplers.

Passenger accommodation was similar to the Class 455 EMU design. Each vehicle had two bi-parting sliding doors on each side for passenger use. The doors were under the overall control of the guard but were locally operated. Double-glazed windows were fitted with tinted glass to reduce glare.

The heating system used waste heat from the engines. Heaters were mounted under the seats, and warm air distribution was assisted by fans. The system was supplemented by an oil-fired water heater. Ventilators were incorporated in the roof, and air circulation was aided by hinged twin-hopper windows during warm weather.

Lighting was by undiffused fluorescent tubes placed longitudinally in each vehicle. Seating saloons were segregated from door vestibules by draught screens incorporating toughened glass. A lockable parcels area was provided in one vehicle of each set, with tip-up seats to give passenger accommodation if needed.

On the prototype trains two different seating types were fitted. The first had bus-type seats with a mix of unidirectional and facing bays. Seating was for 252 with a crush loading capacity of 617. The middle vehicle of set No 150002 had BR's inner-suburban seating.

The 150 design was sufficiently flexible to accept a wide range of different seating from bench seats to InterCity standard, and the

Left: After initial introduction and commissioning, the two prototype Class 150/0 sets, Nos 150001 and 150002, were frequently used on the Derby to Matlock route, where they remained close to the Railway Technical Centre while being in revenue earning service. On 10 July 1986 set No 150001 is seen at Ambergate forming the 17.48 Derby to Matlock service. **Author**

ratio of seats to standing space could be varied to suit individual operating requirements.

A modular toilet compartment was fitted on one vehicle of each unit.

The layout of the driver's cab was similar to that used on previous recent multiple unit designs. The cab had no external doors, with a central door feeding a transverse vestibule, this did take up valuable seating space and at the official launch, the then BR Provincial Director John Edmonds said that the BRB were to seek union agreement to adopt a new design with seats going right up to the front windows on the offside for subsequent builds – however this was not to be.

The prototype Class 150 sets were allocated to Derby Etches Park depot and operated extensive trials on services between Derby and Matlock. The sets soon became known as 'Sprinters'. Livery for the

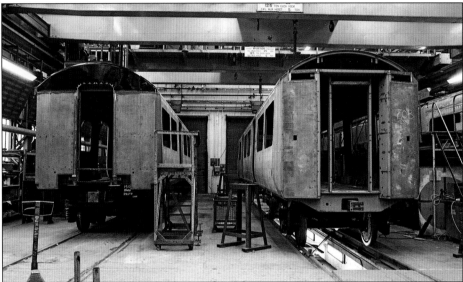

Top: *Assembly of the 50 two-car Class 150/1 sets was a rapid affair, with major resources set aside for the project at BREL York Works, where assembly was alongside the Class 317, 318 and 455 stock. On 5 February 1986 sets Nos 150141 and 150140 are seen in the works yard receiving final static tests before delivery to Derby Etches Park.* **Author**

Right: *By February 1986 the first body shell for a Class 150/2 was under test at York Works and is seen here on the left next to a Class 318 vehicle. This shell was assembled in advance of the normal build to allow for testing.* **Author**

Below: *On 25 May 1985 set No 150002 was used to form charter services over the Worksworth branch, diverging off the main line at Duffield. The set awaits departure from Worksworth with the 14.37 to Derby.* **John Tuffs**

prototype units was Provincial two-tone blue/white/light grey.

In November 1984 the authorisation was given to build a further fleet of 50 sets, classified as 150/1, which were two-car sets. The order was worth £25 million and assembly was again contracted to BREL York works. Except for a modified livery, the original design was closely followed. Sets were gangwayed only at the inner end thus restricting passenger and guard movement whilst the train was in motion.

By 20 January 1986, 37 of the new 'Sprinters' had replaced almost all the old DMUs in the East Midlands, this being some three months earlier than originally planned. Initially there was to have been no 'phasing-in' period. All 50 of the first production batch were to have entered service at once, throughout the Midlands and North and mid-Wales from May 1986. However, due to smart work by BREL York, enough of the design were ready to enable the old first generation DMUs to be replaced from January 1986. From that date the 37 commissioned 'Sprinter' sets based at Derby Etches Park took over all the services on the Lincoln-Nottingham/Birmingham/Crewe, Leicester-Birmingham and Derby-Matlock routes. Some of the class also worked to Grantham and Peterborough. In March 1986 an official launch of their class took place on the Cambrian lines in mid-Wales.

By late 1985 agreement had been reached between central Government and the BRB to build a further fleet of two-car 'Sprinter' sets, classified 150/2; these would have full train length gangways enabling staff and passengers to have full train access.

This work entailed some major structural re-engineering providing a front end more in keeping with the final two tranches of Southern Region Class 455s. The cab was totally redesigned to occupy just a one third width. The slam style cab vestibule doors were replaced with a single leaf sliding unit, this was also available for passenger access. The passenger environment was much in keeping with the earlier design sets.

As the design incorporated major structural changes a prototype body shell

Above: *Displaying the original Provincial 'Sprinter' livery of two-tone light and dark blue off-set by white bands, set No 150115 departs from Wakefield Westgate on 24 April 1989 with a service from Derby to Leeds.* **Author**

Left: *Some of the first refurbishing of the 'Sprinter' fleet was carried out by West Midlands operator Centro starting in October 1990, when slightly revised interiors and a new livery was applied in an overhaul programme carried out at Tyseley depot. The first set to be completed was No 150116 which was shown off to passenger user groups and the media at Birmingham Snow Hill on 5 October 1990.* **Author**

Second Generation DMUs

was produced in January/February 1986 for structural testing, with the first set, carrying the number 150201 emerging on 20 September 1986. The unit went direct to the Engineering Development Unit at Derby for type testing and entered passenger traffic soon after.

In an interesting livery development the first handful of Class 150/2 deliveries emerged without full yellow ends, having a light grey finish with just yellow applied to the central gangway door.

A total of 85 Class 150/2s were built, allocated to virtually all areas of the network apart from the Southern Region. The sets

were well accepted and performed extremely well.

Over the ensuing 20 plus years the fleets have seen some change. The original prototype sets were later modified as three-car Class 150/1 type units and are now operated by the London Midland franchise on Birmingham area Centro work.

The Class 150/1 sets have seen some change; a number have been modified to become three-car units in the 1500xx number series for London Midland (Centro) use by the addition of a Class 150/2 vehicle coupled between the 150/1 cars. The remaining two-car sets are today operated by London

Midland, Transport for London, FirstGroup and Northern.

The Class 150/2 sets have all seen major refurbishment since original introduction and many now sport state-of-the-art interiors in the 2+2 mode. Sets are operated by Northern, Arriva Trains Wales, London Midland and First Great Western.

A wide cross-section of liveries has been carried following privatisation in 1996 and the transfer of ownership of the '150' fleet to Porterbrook and Angel Trains; the ever-changing ownership has brought some 30 different schemes. A selection is shown in the following pages. ●

Above: *Deployment on the Cambrian line from Shrewsbury to Aberystwyth and Pwllheli commenced in March 1986 and required the fitting of Radio Electronic Token Block (RETB) equipment. On 26 March 1990, sets Nos 150120 and 150109 pass Sutton Bridge Junction, Shrewsbury forming the 09.20 Birmingham New Street to Aberystwyth.* **Author**

Right: *Passenger loading figures in the Birmingham (Centro) area by the late 1980s required a rethink of operations. No extra funding was available to buy extra trains and the only way to strengthen existing services was to reform the two-car Class 150/1s with one car from a disbanded Class 150/2. The 150/2 vehicle having gangways at either end allowing passengers and staff full access through a 'new' three-car set. On 14 September 1992, set No 150130 shunts between duties at Hereford after arriving with the 11.30 from Birmingham New Street.* **Author**

Left: While BREL York works built the entire Class 150 fleet, the site did not carry out any repair operations, this was left to facilities in Derby and Crewe or the private sector Workshops. Looking more like a Christmas parcel than a train, the bodyshell of vehicle 52138 from set No 150138 in viewed in the Derby Litchurch Lane paint shop totally stripped and ready for an application of two-pack paint on 31 March 1992. **Author**

Middle: In 1992 the Greater Manchester PTE, in conjunction with the Regional Railways passenger sector launched a 'Manchester' livery, which was applied to a handful of sets. Consisting of a dark brown base and a grey upper panel, the colours were separated by a red and white band. In immaculate ex-works condition, set No 150133 is seen at Manchester Piccadilly on 7 January 1992. **Author**

Below: The now defunct Central Trains franchise which disappeared with the November 2007 franchise re-mapping, carried out a refurbishment of several of its Class 150 three-car sets in spring-summer 2006, providing a better interior and merging the 150/1 and 150/2 vehicles together as one unit. Set No No 150017 is seen emerging from Tyseley Depot on 15 March 2006. **Brian Morrison**

Second Generation DMUs

Above: *When the first of the gangway fitted Class 150/2s emerged from York Works at the tail end of 1986, a revision to the standard livery was made, with the yellow end being replaced by a predominantly grey end with just the central gangway door finished in yellow. After a short time this livery was abandoned in favour of the full yellow warning end. Carrying the short lived livery variant set No 150230 forms the rear unit of the 14.03 Liverpool Lime Street to Scarborough, made up of three Class 150/2s seen passing Marsden on 19 March 1987.* **Author**

Right: *The standard Regional Railways blue and grey colour, offset by a waist-height turquoise and white band became the standard livery for the Class 150/2 fleet. Here one of the West of England allocation, No 150234 departs from Torquay on 5 October 2002 forming the 14.14 Exeter Central to Paignton all-stations service.* **Author**

Above: *Painted in Wales and West-branded Regional Railways livery, set No 150237 passes Lympstone Village on the Exeter to Exmouth branch on 3 October 2002. The Class 150/2 sets were well accepted by both passengers and staff and in their 20+ years of front-line operation have returned a very high miles per casualty figure.* **Author**

Left: *With privatisation came the launch of a number of new and sometimes rather unusual liveries. Arriva Trains Wales decided to paint some of their Class 150/2s in a two-tone scheme which saw one car painted in green and one in red, with pictogram advertising panels applied to the centre section. Showing this somewhat bizarre scheme, set No 150282 descends Whiteball bank on 25 May 2005 forming a Cardiff Central to Exeter all stations service.* **Author**

Second Generation DMUs

Right: *Class 150/2 driving cab. All variants of the design had the same basic equipment and positions. On the left of the flat desk is the brake controller, with the power (throttle) handle on the right side. The main instrumentation and switch gear is on the angled panel, while the cab to cab and public address telephone is attached to the front facing bulkhead. Since original introduction a number of extra fittings have been made to the cab, including cab secure radio, (handset and radio on left side wall), driver's reminder appliance (on left wall in front of window), TPWS (located above window height to the left of the destination indicator) and a cab cooling fan on the right almost out of view. The cab illustrated is from FGW set No 150247.* **Author**

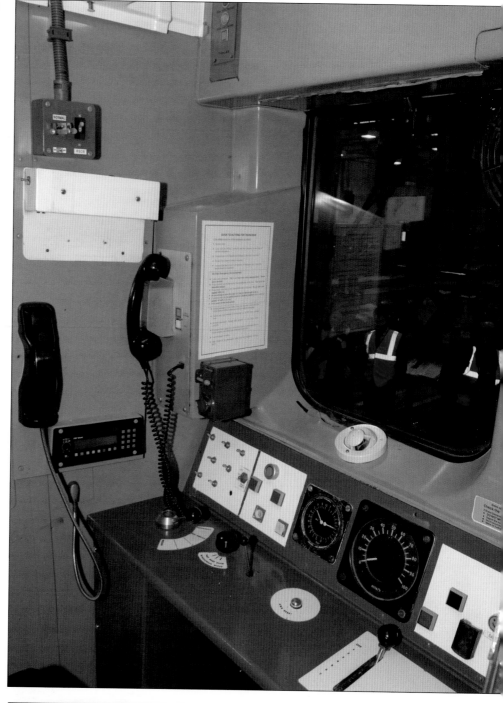

Right: *Another of the shorter-lived local Regional Railways liveries was this yellow and white, offset by a waist-height black and grey band. The colours were applied to some sets working in the Merseyrail area. Set No 150207 is seen in the bay platform at Stockport in spring 1992.* **Author**

Above: *The Wessex Trains franchise was one of the first to use a pictogram livery, when their entire fleet of Class 150/2 sets was painted in a base maroon scheme and then each set given unique picture branding, many associated with line of route advertising. Some people thought the livery a little overpowering and nothing more than official graffiti, while others found the scheme pleasing to the eye. On 6 August 2006, sets Nos 150236 and 150265 pass Cockwood Harbour forming the 17.48 Paignton to Exmouth service.* **Author**

Below: *The present Arriva Trains Wales franchise has adopted a rather pleasing turquoise and stone colour scheme for its entire fleet. The livery is shown here on set No 150279 at Cardiff Central. All Arriva Trains sets have now been fully refurbished with 2+2 seating.* **Author**

Below: *First Great Western, which had its franchise enlarged from April 2006 when it took over the London area suburban network and the previous Wessex Trains operation, became the operator of a sizeable Class 150 fleet, jointly allocated between Bristol St Philips Marsh and Exeter depots. A major refurbishing scheme commenced in 2007 with Pullman Rail at Cardiff carrying out a significant interior makeover with many new components. On the outside, the trains are now in the FirstGroup 'Dynamic Lines' livery, with the stripes of the lower panel being replaced by names of local FGW served areas, local attractions and community groups. On 5 April 2007, set No 150249 passes along the Dawlish Sea Wall at Rockstone Bridge forming the 09.14 Paignton to Exmouth service. The West Country local services in the Exeter area have now been taken over by ex-Northern Class 142 'Pacer' sets which has not been welcomed by passengers, user groups or staff.* **Author**

In March 1983, the then British Railways Board Provincial Sector decided to order two prototype medium distance conventional DMU trains from two different manufacturers. In the previous section we have looked at what rapidly became the 'standard' BR produced unit, but in this section we look at what was possibly at the time the most stylish DMU ever to operate on British rails, the Metro-Cammell Class 151.

Unlike the BREL prototypes of Class 150, these Class 151 prototypes were unfortunately late in delivery and even before completion Metro-Cammell encountered problems with the trade unions over the design and layout of the driving cabs and guard accommodation. Delays while changes were made, led to the first Class 151 not arriving at Derby for trials until February 1985; meanwhile fleet building of the rival Class 150 from BREL had already begun - despite lack of time to test and compare the two alternative prototypes.

The rapid ordering without proven trials was due to the urgent need to replace existing asbestos-contaminated DMUs. The replacement programme gathered pace, and in 1985 the Government authorised another 240 'Sprinters' type DMUs. Many thought this would go to Metro-Cammell following the BRBs quest to split large orders, however this was not to be and it quickly became evident that the Class 151 was already out of the running for further 'Sprinter'

orders. Instead it was announced, Metro-Cammell would be involved in the design and construction of the new 23m DMU, which later became the Class 156. Viewed against this early rejection of the '151' for production it remains that the design was superior to its BREL Class 150 rival, in particular in the layout of the seats and bodyside windows.

In technical terms the aluminium-bodied Class 151 three-car sets saw each car carried on two four-wheel bogies by an air bag-type secondary suspension. Primary suspension comprised of rubber chevrons by each axle box. Each car had both axles of one bogie powered, and the three cars of each unit were coupled by semi-permanent bar-couplers, gangways were provided between vehicles, but not at the driving ends. Access to the passenger compartment was by two pairs of pneumatically-operated sliding leaf doors on each car side. The door control circuit and interlocks provide for one or two-man operation or passenger control of doors released by staff.

Each car was fitted with one underframe-mounted Cummins NT 855-R4 engine rated at 285bhp. The cooling system was connected in a 'closed circuit' with a header tank positioned such that the minimum level in the tank will be above the highest point in the circuit. Coolant was topped up from an underframe-mounted reserve tank. This allowed for re-filling of the header tank from the trackside

by means of an electrically-driven pump.

The sets had a hydro-mechanical transmission with a single-stage hydro-kinetic torque converter associated with a three-speed bi-directional gearbox.

The interior layout of the sets was in the 3+2 high-density style, using low-back seats which tied in perfectly with the window positions. All seating was in standard class style, small above seat luggage racks were provided with lino-covered floors. The three-car sets were formed Driving Motor Standard seating 80, Motor Standard seating 84 and Driving Motor Standard Lavatory seating 68. A high-quality communication system was installed providing a public address system of direct messages with the ability to add pre-recorded messages as time progressed. A cab to cab communication system was also fitted.

The body styling of the Class 151s was very pleasing with deep front windows more in keeping with mainland European styles of the period. Both Class 151 sets were delivered in unpainted aluminium finish, with the bold lining of the then new two-tone blue and white of the Provincial Services Sector.

The first Class 151, numbered 151001 was delivered to Derby in January 1985 and commenced a series of very detailed static and dynamic tests, these involving runs on the Mickleover and Old Dalby test tracks as well as runs over the main line to Leicester, Bedford and St Pancras. The second of the

Below: *In common with all new rolling stock deliveries of the era, be it multiple units, locomotives, coaches or wagons, the type test approval and certification process was carried out by the Engineering Development Unit (EDU) at the Railway Technical Centre, Derby. After being hauled from the Metro-Cammell Works in Birmingham to Derby in June 1985, the set is seen in the EDU yard on 12 August 1985 awaiting entry into the test hall for instrumentation. On the left is a Mk3 sleeper which was also part of an ongoing type test programme at the time.* **Author**

build was kept at the Birmingham works of Metro-Cammell for many months and did not arrive at Derby until June 1985, not officially being taken into stock until January 1986, but was in operation well before that date.

As part of the type test programme, the Class 151s were reduced to two-car formations at various times for both test and passenger services. The vast majority of passenger work was on the Derby – Matlock route, but runs to Birmingham, Crewe, Sheffield and Manchester were not uncommon. One of the most notable passenger workings was on 21 September 1985 when set No 151001 operated the 'shuttle' passenger service between Swansea station and Landore depot for the Great Western 150 Open Day.

To avoid confusion with numbering of the Class 150 fleet, the '151s' were renumbered in February 1988 as 151003 and 151004. The pair remained available for service until March 1989 when both sets were withdrawn and stored at Derby.

After periods of store at Derby, Llandudno Junction and Blackpool, the two sets were transferred to the ownership of Railtest, later Serco Railtest for conversion into test trains, but this never materialised, mainly due to most of the components being non-standard and the wish to re-bogie the sets with conventional 'Sprinter' bogies being impossible without huge structural alterations. In 2000 the six vehicles were sold to Endeavour Rail who moved the vehicles to store at Crewe. It was then planned to pass the vehicles through the LNWR works at Crewe and return the sets to front line passenger service, offering them to TOCs on an 'ad-hoc' hire basis. However, this never came to fruition and in 2004 the sets were broken up at Crewe. ●

Above: *Due to the complexity of the Class 151 design a higher than usual number of dynamic tests were performed before passenger certification was granted. On 11 July 1985, set No 151001 pulls off the Sinfin branch at Peartree south of Derby while forming a Derby-Sinfin-Matlock test run. The roof mounted heaters and radiators are clearly visible in this view.* **John Tuffs**

Left: *During the early main line testing period of both the Class 150 and 151 prototype units, runs were made, usually at night, between Derby and London St Pancras. This undated view, probably taken in early 1986 shows Metro-Cammell No 151001 and BREL No 150001 under the Barlow roof at St Pancras.* **Ken Brunt**

Left: *By spring 1986 both the Class 151s could be found operating on the Derby to Matlock route. Good passenger operating experience could be obtained with frequent station stops and moderate passenger loadings. The close proximity to the Engineering Development Unit at Derby meant that their deployment on this route was low risk, as if a major problem was experienced help was quickly at hand. In reality very few operating problems were recorded. On 1 April 1986 set No 151002 approaches Duffield from Milford Tunnel with a Matlock to Derby service.* **John Tuffs**

Below: *It was soon found that the unpainted aluminium body of the Class 151s looked scruffy; however the bodies were never painted, except for the yellow warning ends and the application of Provincial Sector blue and white stripes on the bodysides. Running with what appears to be the cab sliding door in an open position, set No 151002 departs from Duffield and heads to Derby with the 09.20 service from Matlock on 1 April 1986.* **John Tuffs**

Above: *By 1987 the operating area for the Class 151s was slightly expanded. Still allocated to Derby Etches Park, the sets could be found working to Birmingham and Crewe. Here on 14 November 1987, set No 151002 makes the scheduled stop at Water Orton with a Derby to Birmingham New Street service. The operating range of the '151s' was restricted by the fact that only Derby drivers and guards were trained on their operation.* **John Tuffs**

Middle: *Stabled in one of the middle platform lines at Derby Midland station, set No 151001 awaits departure to Matlock in mid-1986. Although the crew doors entering the full width cab/guards area were of the sliding type, these were not powered but hand-operated with an interlock facility to secure closure.* **Kevin Wills**

Right: *By some standards, the interior of the Class 151s were quite spartan, with considerable use of melamine surfaces and bland wall spaces without glazed panels by door positions. However, with window positions lining up by seat locations this improved the overall perception of the vehicle interiors. The ceiling panels were predominantly flat with a centre light cluster running the entire length of the vehicles including through the door areas. Each window had an opening hopper. Seats were of the low-back moquette covered type with single grab handles rather than poles. The floor was covered in moulded lino.* **Keith Grafton**

As part of the BRBs quest to reduce the cost of operations on lightly used branch lines, especially in rural areas, a study was made in the 1980s with the desire to introduce a new generation of single car units, replacing the first generation members of Class 121 and 122.

Rather than build new trains, it was decided to convert the 35 members of the Class 155 fleet operated by the Provincial sector into 70 single car sets classified as 153 at a cost of £9m.

Originally built by Leyland at their Workington factory, the rebuild contract was put out to competitive tender, with the work being won by Hunslet-Barclay of Kilmarnock, a company at the time with detailed knowledge of the modern BR multiple unit fleet, having built the underframes for the Class 143s and successfully executed the major upgrade/refurbishment of the Class 141 fleet.

The rebuilding of the Class 155s into 153s was a complex affair; the former 'inner' end of the coach had to be totally rebuilt and within the confines of the existing body structure provide a driving cab of comparative quality to the original Leyland cab. This was no easy operation as the space between the door position and end panels was much less, this resulting in a very compact cab slightly protruding into the door pocket area. The cab was difficult to enter by more portly footplate staff and was the subject of major complaints when the sets were first introduced.

A new cab exterior was fabricated to replace the original inner end, which due to a number of restricting factors of structural rigidity was not exactly the same as the original design, thus rendering the train with two slightly different driving ends.

A number of other structural changes had to be made, including the fitting of standard automatic couplers at the 'new' end and providing a within vehicle space for the exhaust pipe to reach a roof exit position.

The passenger interior was kept much the same as in Class 155 days, using 2+2 seating, with a toilet at one end with a secure stowage area opposite.

The new units were numbered in the range 153301-153335 and 153351-153385, with individual cars numbered 52301-335 and 57351-385 (this later group were originally numbered 57301-335), but changed to avoid numeric clashes.

The first vehicle to be completed at Kilmarnock, carrying the then new Regional Railways livery, No 153354, was sent to the Engineering Development Unit at Derby in May 1991 with an official launch to the media of the fleet at the Hunslet-Barclay factory on 18 July 1991 when guests were invited to travel on a set between the Kilmarnock Works, Ayr and Carlisle.

When converted the Class 153s were destined for use in Cumbria, North Yorkshire, Lincolnshire, East Anglia, Wales and the West Country. Upon the mid 1990s privatisation, the '153s' became split between several operators and in 2008 the fleet is operated by Arriva Trains Wales (eight vehicles), East Midlands Trains (17 vehicles), London Midland (10 vehicles), Northern Rail (18 vehicles), National Express Anglia (five vehicles) and First Great Western (12 vehicles). ●

Below: *At the height of the Class 155-153 conversion project at Hunslet Barclay of Kilmarnock, around 10 individual vehicles were under modification at the same time. All were operated to and from the works under their own power. On 18 July 1991 unit No 153314 is seen at an advanced stage of modification with its new cab fitted and cosmetic attention progressing. On the right is one of six operational Hunslet Barclay Class 20/9 locomotives used for contract weed control work for Chipmans.* **Author**

Above: *Viewed from its 'new' end, Class 153 No 153317, converted from the 52xxx vehicle from Class 155 No 155317 stands in the main erecting shop at Hunslet Barclay on 18 July 1991. This vehicle was used for the official launch, being driven through a banner from the works enclosed paint booth to the main shop in front of over 100 guests. It is quite amazing that the space between the edge of the door pocket and body end provides enough room for the cab and guard's accommodation.* **Author**

Below: *One of the first areas to benefit from the use of Class 153s was the Cumbrian coast line, at the time providing sufficient accommodation for passenger demands on the route. On 12 August 1996, set No 153367 arrives at Workington with the 09.00 service to Carlisle. The vehicle's original '155' cab is leading, being always recognisable in having the lamp clusters at the base of the bodywork, while the revised cab has the lamp clusters mid-height up the body.* **Author**

Left: *Following privatisation from 1996 the Class 153s remained operational with a number of companies, many of which have 'changed' in the 1996-2008 period. In the main however, the fleet has remained on rural lines or routes of low patronage. Painted in Arriva Trains turquoise livery, set No 153352 shunts between platforms at Sheffield on 28 August 2002. This unit was converted from Class 155 No 155302, the second set of the original built. Viewed from its small cab end, note the National Radio Network radio aerials on the cab roof.* **Author**

Left: *Since original conversion, the Class 153s have always been found operating in Wales and the West Country. In Devon and Cornwall the fleet has been one of the sources of traction for branch line use, where operations have generally been single units, while busier services through Devon have frequently been formed of two or even three Class 153s coupled together. In the period of the Wales & West train operating company three distinct liveries were adopted, black for vehicles supported by the Devon & Cornwall Rail Partnership, orange for sets working on West Wales routes and red for units allocated to Wessex duties on the Bristol-Southampton/Weymouth route. With franchise alterations, areas of deployment changed and by 2004/5 the orange (Wales) sets were confined to Welsh operations working for Arriva, while the red and black sets became a common pool working for Wessex and later First Great Western. On 3 August 2004, a Devon and Cornwall Rail Partnership 'black' and Wessex 'red' Class 153 depart from Dawlish forming the 16.24 Exmouth to Paignton, while in the distance a Class 180 approaches with the 14.35 Paddington to Plymouth service.* **Author**

Second Generation DMUs

The St. Ives Bay Belle

Top: *Many people criticised the use of single-car trains on the more popular Devon branches, but for off-peak and non-school services the accommodation was sufficient. Painted in Devon & Cornwall Rail Partnership black and gold livery, set No 153374 is seen near Lympstone Village on the Exeter to Exmouth branch on 3 October 2002 forming the 13.52 Exeter St Davids to Exmouth.* **Author**

Right and Inset: *Just a few months before the Wessex franchise was transferred to First Great Western in April 2006, two of the West of England Class 153s were repainted into light blue pictogram liveries in support of the St Ives and Looe branches in an attempt by the Devon & Cornwall Rail Partnership to promote the important tourist routes. Set No 153329 was rolled out to the media and passenger user groups in St Ives livery on 4 December 2005 and is seen right passing Carbis Bay forming the 14.12 St Ives to Penzance. Prior to forming the service the unit was officially named The St. Ives Bay Belle with a stick-on style plate, shown in the inset above. Both:* **Author**

Left: *Painted in First North Western blue and gold star livery, but in 2007 operating for Arriva Trains Wales, set No 153310 is seen at Cardiff General on 5 November 2007 while undertaking drivers' route training. This view is taken from the original Class 155 end; from the body side this can be immediately identified as the end with glazed windows right up to the door pocket.* **Author**

Middle: *As part of First Great Western's franchise commitment in 2006, the Class 153 sets had to be fully refurbished. This work was contracted to Wabtec Rail, who also won the Class 158 refurbishment contract. The physical work on the Class 153s was undertaken at Wabtec's Eastleigh site, a part of the former Southern workshop. The sets have emerged with new 2+2 seating in a very cramped configuration with high backs in which portly passengers have a job to sit. Outside, the coaches have been finished in FirstGroup's Dynamic Lines livery in a similar style to the Class 150s and 158s. Set No 153368 is seen at Cogload Junction, Taunton on 26 January 2008 forming a transit move to Exeter Depot.* **Brian Garrett**

Below: *Many depots have had an association with the Class 153 fleet over the years, while various major workshops such as Doncaster, Crewe and Glasgow have performed overhauls. Today, under the control of the private sector more attention is carried out by owning depots with less emphasis on major workshops for attention. However, the Class 153s were in 2008 receiving major attention by Wabtec. Displaying the Wessex Weymouth livery, set No 153370 is seen 'on shed' at Exeter on 4 July 2006 in the company of a Class 150 and 158. The Wessex Weymouth livery carefully disguised the solid side window position at one end, using it for a pictogram and branding. The depot facility at Exeter, adjacent to Exeter St Davids station is now operated by First Great Western and looks after members of Classes 142, 150, 153 and 158.* **Author**

Right: When originally converted from Class 155s to 153s, the 'as built' seating was retained; this was a good quality medium-height seat covered in grey and red chevron moquette, having orange tube grab handles mounted above the outer seats. A mix of airline and group seats were provided with hinged corridor side armrests. Total accommodation per vehicle was for 72, plus three tip-up seats. The interior of No 153317 is shown looking towards the No 2 or toilet end. **Author**

Middle: Over the years, especially following privatisation a number of changes to the interior decor have been made, some new seats of the Chapman type, but still to the standard 2+2 configuration have been installed. In most cases the newer sets incorporate grab handles above each seat with an individual seat number. This is the interior of a 'one' Anglia vehicle, again looking towards the No 2 or toilet end. **Author**

Right: Described by Regional Railways at the time of the Class 153 launch as a 'space saver' cab, the small new cab was quite a masterpiece of engineering in trying to fit the physical desk, pipework, electrical switch gear and other equipment into a very small area. The size of the cab was a slight problem with the drivers' trade union ASLE&F at the time, especially when only the dimensions were advised to the union and no actual cab was available for inspection. However all parties worked well together and some refinements were made to provide a cab largely acceptable to all. The power controller (or throttle as it is marked on the desk) is operated by the driver's right hand, while the five-step brake controller is operated by his left hand. Three dials are provided on the angular panel, giving brake pipe pressure, speed and brake cylinder pressure. On the main panel the switchgear used press button and rotary controls, while the windscreen wiper valve, AWS reset button and warning air horn valve are located on the flat section of the desk. The driver's safety device (DSD) or dead man's pedal is located on an angled panel in the floor. **Author**

11 Class 154

The classification '154' covers just one unit, which was actually the second of the BREL 'prototype' Class 150/0 sets No 150002 built in 1984 to establish the standard second-generation DMU. Set No 150002 was originally fitted with Rolls Royce engines (later changed to Perkins), a Self Changing Gears transmission and Gmeinder final drives. Unfortunately this was not totally successful and the set, allocated to Derby, was selected to evaluate a number of traction innovations and modifications.

Following original trials, it was withdrawn from passenger service as a Class 150 and fitted with Twin Disc hydraulic 'hot shift' gearboxes which were equipped with a new control system. These gearboxes were of the type originally fitted to the prototype Class 151s and had not been considered suitable for further rail use. Modification work was undertaken at the EDU Derby and 154001 was officially certified in January 1987.

To distinguish the trial set from the normal Class 150, it was agreed to reclassify the unit as '154' and renumber it 154001. The set was allocated to Derby Etches Park and used on normal 'Sprinter' duties. In February 1988 the unit was again renumbered, to 154002.

The set was later selected to take part in traction development and air conditioning trials of equipment projected for fitting to the proposed Class 158s for use in Scotland. New heating and ventilation was installed and the set regeared for 90mph operation.

The Class 154 operated a number of test trains in the Midlands as well as passenger carrying services based at Derby. As part of its test programme in conjunction with the Class 158 design, the set also operated in Scotland.

After the trials were complete, No 154001 was totally rebuilt as a standard Class 150/0 three-car set and is now operating as set No 150002. ●

Below: *Carrying the small yellow warning end applied to the two BREL prototype units when built, the development set now numbered 154002 passes Peartree, south of Derby on 23 May 1989 forming a Derby to Birmingham service. By the time this picture was taken, showing the set running with its toilet fitted DMS leading, cab roof aerials for the cab radio system had been installed.* **Author**

Right: *With its air conditioning vents on the roof of the driving cars, set No 154002, running in its correct three-car formation, is seen just north of Burton-on Trent on 1 March 1988. At the time the set was forming the 10.07 Derby to Birmingham, but due to an operating problem on the outskirts of Birmingham the train was terminated at Burton-on-Trent.* **John Tuffs**

Below: *During part of its test programme, the middle motor second was removed at various times with the set operating as a two car; this occurred during passenger running in both England and Scotland. Carrying its number 154001, the set is seen at Matlock on 21 March 1987, soon after conversion forming the 14.58 passenger service to Nottingham via Derby.* **John Tuffs**

Concurrent with the announcement from the BRB of the ordering of the second batch of Class 150 units (classified 150/2) came the notification that on 15 January 1985 an order for 35 two-car 'Super Sprinter' type units with 75ft body shells had been ordered from Leyland at a value of £125m. These sets were destined for the Cardiff area to replace ageing longer-distance DMUs on routes such as the Cardiff to Birmingham/Manchester, Portsmouth, Brighton, Weymouth and West of England lines, where the high-density of the previously ordered types would not be suitable.

This order from Leyland was classified as 155 and were low-density main line style sets, having 2+2 seating, toilets and increased luggage locker space, as at the time the BR Parcels business under the Red Star name was trying to improve its business.

Unlike the previous products from Leyland, the Class 155s were to be fully built at Leyland in Workington and delivered to the RTC Derby as fully functional trains.

The body sections were again based on the bus assembly style, formed of modules attached to a common underframe. The interiors (full railway width) used a pleasing style with a mix of group and airline layout of traditional railway seats. A toilet was located in each vehicle at the inner end with a parcels locker opposite. A one-third-width driving cab was provided with an end gangway enabling sets to operate in multiple.

Assembly commenced in Workington in 1986 with the first set No 155301 emerging in Spring 1987, when the set was transferred to the EDU at Derby for type test approval. Main line testing was conducted at first in the Mickleover and Old Dalby test tracks followed by the LM main line, but by 4 August 1987 set No 155301 worked from Derby to Bristol via Oxford for a series of tests over the Bristol-Didcot line.

The 35 sets were allocated to Cardiff and soon after introduction started to cause major problems with gauging and door issues to a degree that at one time the entire fleet was grounded and replacement Class 156s drafted into the area. However problems were resolved, but to many these were the worst of the modern DMU 'Sprinter' types, largely due to there having been no prototype built to iron out design and operational problems.

The power unit installed under each vehicle was a Cummins NT855 R5 of 286hp driving a Voith final drive.

In 1990 it was agreed that the rail industry would benefit from 70 single car sets rather than 35 two-car units and agreement was reached for the Class 155s to be rebuilt as Class 153s by Hunslet-Barclay of Kilmarnock.

In 1988 an order was placed for a further seven Class 155s, funded by West Yorkshire PTE for use on the Caldervale line. These sets, which still remain in service today, had only one toilet per set and were fitted out with a revised interior.

Assembly was again carried out at Workington, body finish was in WYPTE maroon and buttermilk and sets were allocated to Leeds Neville Hill. These seven sets have in more recent years been fully refurbished and now operate under the Northern Rail franchise banner painted in Northern maroon and blue pictogram livery. ●

Below: As part of the rigorous type test approval process, following static testing at the Engineering Development Unit at Derby, dynamic testing was carried out on the two test tracks as well as on the main line. In addition to running over the Midland route, the Class 155s and 156s were trialled over the Derby-Birmingham-Oxford-Swindon-Bristol route. On 5 August 1987, the first unit of the fleet No 155301 approaches Foxall Junction, Didcot with the 10.34 Bristol Temple Meads to Didcot test special. **Author**

Right: *Awaiting dispatch from the Leyland factory in Workington, set No 155301 shows its 'as delivered' condition, painted in then standard BR Provincial grey and blue livery, offset by a turquoise and white body band and the Sprinter legend on the body side. It is interesting to note the Leyland logo applied below the non-driving front window, this historic iconic 'badge' clearly telling the public who built the trains. Perhaps, with hindsight, impending problems meant that this was not such a good move. The Leyland name was not carried by other sets, but remained on No 155301 for several years.* **Author's Collection**

Below: *Although the Class 155s were problematical to the operators, the sets seemed to find favour with passengers, and during a survey some 75 per cent of travellers on the Manchester-Crewe-Cardiff route preferred to travel on a Class 155 than existing loco-hauled or other multiple unit types. On 26 March 1990 set No 155330 passes Sutton Bridge Junction, Shrewsbury forming the 08.21 Manchester Piccadilly to Cardiff service.* **Author**

Above: *The Cardiff/Bristol to the far West of England line was an ideal route for the Class 155s, offering a pleasing passenger environment and low-density 2+2 seating. Traversing the Sea Wall at Horse Cove, set No 155311 heads west on 15 April 1991 forming the 11.56 Swindon to Paignton service. This set was taken out of traffic the following week for conversion into two Class 153s.* **Author**

Below: *Forming the 13.05 Brighton, Portsmouth and Southampton to Cardiff service, set No 153312 departs from Severn Tunnel Junction station on the final leg of its run to the Welsh capital on 9 April 1991.* **Author**

Above: *The seven West Yorkshire PTE or Metro Class 155s were very similar to the mainstream Provincial fleet, except that only one toilet was fitted per train and the exterior was finished in the maroon and buttermilk colours of the operator. Set No 155341 is seen at the ProRail factory at Horbury on 25 May 1996 while some interior refurbishment was being carried out. These sets have always operated from Leeds Neville Hill depot, largely on Caldervale routes.* **Author**

Below: *The seven West Yorkshire PTE sponsored sets, allocated to Leeds Neville Hill depot and operated by Northern were all refurbished in 2006-07 with revised interiors and a new exterior livery based on the Northern style but with route-associated pictograms. On 12 February 2007, set No 155347 passes Walsden while forming the 11.08 Leeds to Manchester Victoria service.* **Mark Bearton**

On 30 October 1985 the British Railways Board announced that a further 228 new-generation 'Sprinter Express' vehicles formed as 114 two-car units had been ordered from Metro-Cammell of Washwood Heath, Birmingham. This order, classified as 156, was for 75ft long vehicles for longer distance use. The interiors were low density and to meet the demands of longer distance travel, single-leaf sliding doors were placed towards vehicle ends, feeding transverse walkways rather than opening directly into the passenger saloon areas.

Assembly of the coach shells was sub-contracted to Procor of Wakefield (118 shells), W. H. Davis (60 shells) and Standard Wagon (50 shells); each then transported the completed pre-painted structures by road to Washwood Heath for assembly.

The first 100 sets, allocated numbers 156401-156500 were funded by the BR Provincial sector, the final 14 sets Nos 156501-156514 were funded by Strathclyde Passenger Transport Executive. Provincial sets were finished in grey/blue livery, while Strathclyde sets were painted in orange and brown.

The first set ,No 156401, was tested between Washwood Heath and Banbury on 10 November 1987 and was transferred to the EDU at the Railway Technical Centre, Derby

on 4 December 1987 for type test approval. The second set of the fleet, No 156402, was delivered direct to Norwich depot for training and passenger use in early January 1988. The set was subsequently transferred to Scotland for demonstration purposes and a '156' carried fare paying passengers for the first time on 26 January 1988 when set No 156402 formed the 11.35 Inverness to Wick.

During the course of the build, Metro-Cammell was sold to Alstom with effect from 26 May 1989; with the final sets technically built by Alstom, the final set, No 156514, was delivered to Scotland on 28 September 1989.

The interior of the sets was pleasing to the public, with a mix of airline and group seats in the 2+2 style. One toilet was provided per set, and units were gangwayed throughout, allowing trains of up to 12-car formation to operate. A small lock-up parcels area was provided and a one-third-width driving cab was fitted.

The standard 'Sprinter' power unit - the Cummins NT855 R5 of 285hp - was installed below each coach, with traction passing via a Voith transmission.

The first deliveries of Class 156s went to Norwich for use on East Anglia-Midland and North West services. Next came Scotland, replacing loco-hauled services on South East

Scotland and on the West Highland line, the Aberdeen, Wick and Thurso lines.

In December 1988 the entire Class 155 fleet were grounded and a number of Class 156s were drafted into Cardiff from Scotland to operate services to Brighton via Southampton, some Class 156s remained working from Cardiff until November 1989.

Other new deliveries took units to Leeds Neville Hill for TransPennine use and of course the final sets to Glasgow for Strathclyde work.

Upon privatisation the Class 156s were split between two lease companies, Porterbrook who had 38 units and Angel Trains 76 sets.

Today, the split of units is between Stagecoach East Midlands (11), National Express Anglia (9), Northern (46) and First ScotRail (48).

In the summer of 1989 in conjunction with the NS50 celebrations in Holland, the UK was invited to send a train for display. Strathclyde Class 156 No 156402 was selected and prepared at the EDU Derby. It was taken under its own power to Dover on 16 June 1989 and travelled via the Dover-Dunkerque train ferry, from where it was driven under its own power to Utrecht. After two weeks on display the set returned to the UK under its own power to the ferry port and once back in Dover it returned to Derby. ●

Below: *Carrying 'Super Sprinter' branding and painted in as-delivered Provincial livery, set No 156468 passes Chinley on 20 July 1989 forming the 10.20 Liverpool Lime Street to Ipswich service. This set was delivered from Metro-Cammell in January 1989. This unit was seriously damaged in a collision with sister set No 156490 at Mallerstang on the Settle & Carlisle line on 31 January 1995. It was subsequently repaired and is now in traffic based at Newton Heath.* **Author**

Above: *Although the construction contract for the Class 156s was awarded to Metro-Cammell, the physical body assembly was sub-contracted to one of three fabrication suppliers, Procor, W. H. Davis and Standard Wagon. Procor's body shell No 112, which is understood to have been finished as part of set No 156456, is seen in the main fabrication shop at the Horbury Junction plant on 25 April 1989.* **Author**

Below: *The fourth set of the build, No 156404 allocated to Norwich is seen on 17 March 1989 when just a few weeks old passing Clay Cross Junction, south of Chesterfield, forming the 12.14 Blackpool North to Cambridge cross-country service. At the time these long-distance services, which did not have many end-to-end customers, offered a trolley catering service.* **Author**

Left: *After deployment on the longer-distance services, the Class 156s soon became popular with passengers, offering a good travelling environment. One of the most significant improvements over other units was that the exterior opening passenger doors fed a transverse walkway rather than directly into the travelling saloon, reducing the loss of heat at station stops and making for a more friendly travelling atmosphere. On 25 May 1989, set No 156452 passes near Duffield, north of Derby, with a service bound for Yarmouth.* **Author**

Right: *The final 14 sets of the build were funded by Strathclyde Passenger Transport Executive and painted in Glasgow orange and brown livery, a colour scheme which looked very smart if kept clean. Purchased for work on the Glasgow-area non-electrified routes, the sets have remained working in their designated area right to the present day, although now painted in carmine and cream livery. Sporting the original application of orange with a black BR double-arrow logo, set No 156510 departs from Glasgow Central on 21 August 1992 with a service bound for Edinburgh via Shotts.* **Author**

Left: *Displaying the ScotRail logo on the bodyside and below the non-driving front window, set No 156507 departs at Kilmarnock on 22 May 1995 with a service bound for Glasgow Central.* **Author**

Second Generation DMUs

Above: *The Strathclyde Passenger Transport Executive changed its livery from orange to carmine and cream in 1996 and the first Class 156 to sport the new colours was No 156433, launched into service on 24 September 1996. The livery is shown here on set No 156500, repainted from provincial colours. This unit is seen arriving at Ayr on 29 August 2002 forming the 14.37 Stranraer to Glasgow Central.* **Author**

Below: *After the BR passenger businesses were split up into small business units prior to full privatisation, the Regional Railways business was launched in December 1990. Repaints to sets after that date emerged in a new and rather distinctive scheme of light and dark grey offset by white and light blue body bands. The dark grey was stylised at the cab ends. Originally the Regional Railways name was applied, but following privatisation this was covered by the new operator's name, in this case Central Trains. Set No 156403 is seen at Norwich on 20 June 2003, clearly showing how a different style of paint application can completely change the appearance of a set.* **Author**

Left: *The versatility of the Class 156s and indeed most of the second generation of DMUs is such that cross-coupling is easily possible if vehicles are out of service. In this view we see a two-car set formed of one vehicle from Class 156 No 156412, coupled to Class 153 No 153383. The train, recorded on 23 April 2004 is a Matlock to Derby local service operated by the then Central Trains Co and is viewed near Duffield.* **Author**

Right: *At the time of livery and operator transitions in the 2000-2005 period a number of trains were repainted by their lease owners in 'base' white colour, onto which operator's livery or just a trading title could be added with ease. One such unit was No 156402, the historic member of the '156' fleet as the first passenger-carrying unit back on 26 January 1988. On 23 April 2004 the set is seen at Stenson Junction, between Derby and Burton on Trent, forming a service from Nottingham to Crewe.* **Author**

Left: *It seems that by looking at official records a higher than average number of Class 156s have been involved in serious derailments or collisions. Thankfully all have been repaired and as of late 2008 all sets still remain in traffic. This totally destroyed front end is set 156490, which was involved in a collision with set No 156468 at Mallerstang on the Settle & Carlisle line. On the night of 31 January 1995 set No 156490 was forming the 16.26 Carlisle to Leeds, which had to reverse at Blea Moor due to flooding, soon after restarting it hit a landslip and derailed, landing up in the path of the following 17.45 Carlisle to Leeds formed of set 156468, which had already departed Kirkby Stephen and could not be contacted. The 60mph impact sadly killed the guard who was trying to move his passengers to a point of safety. The damaged vehicle is seen at ABB Derby Litchurch Lane on 13 March 1995 awaiting repair.* **Author**

Second Generation DMUs

Right: *One Railway, owned by National Express and now trading as National Express Anglia, operates a fleet of nine Class 156s based at Norwich Crown Point. In the somewhat garish colours of the operator, No 156416 is seen at Ipswich depot on 28 November 2006. In accordance with the Disability Discrimination Act, all trains must have their passenger doors in a contrasting colour to the general bodywork, to aid partly sighted passengers in finding train access points. In this case a mid green has been chosen.* **Author**

Below: *Advertising liveries have become very popular in recent years providing extra cash for train operators. Several of the 'one' fleet have carried promotional liveries, some reflecting local businesses such as this on set No 156402 advertising the Chapelfield shopping centre in Norwich. Others are used for line promotions involving the Community Rail Partnership.* **Author**

What might have been

When Royal Mail were actively looking at improved methods of transporting letter and parcel traffic by rail, a number of considerations were put forward, using loco-hauled EMU or DMU traction. As time came to prove, the loco-hauled stock was introduced and Class 325 EMUs, but apart from this model nothing was ever furthered of the DMU Royal Mail unit. It was to have been based on the Class 156, with roller shutter doors providing access into stowage vans the same as on Class 325s. The cab was accessed from a transverse walkway and provided no access into the mail-carrying area.

In the late 1980s the British Railways Board under its Provincial sector sought finance to obtain a sizeable fleet of main line DMU stock for the outer suburban or Express routes. Competitive tender saw a substantial order placed with BREL for what became the Class 158, built in either a two or three-car formation.

Much new technology surrounded the Class 158 build, mainly the use of aluminium in vehicle frame and body shell fabrication and the use of disk brakes (the first fitted to a modern DMU fleet).

After the contract was awarded to BREL, the design and assembly work was performed at their Litchurch Lane Works in Derby, where eventually 182 sets comprising 381 vehicles were built; in addition 22 three-car Class 159s were built to identical design giving a fleet size of 447 vehicles.

Assembly of the first set allocated the number 158701 commenced at Derby very early in 1989 and after much construction difficulties the first vehicle was rolled out for the railway press at the RTC Derby on 9 October 1989. At this time the interior was not complete and only the exterior was available for inspection.

Subsequent to the delivery for testing, production was progressing, but soon major problems were discovered in the fabrication, especially with cracks in the aluminium; this was located in the door pockets as well as in the bogie side supports and major rectification had to be carried out before squadron production could progress.

By 1990 most of the assembly problems had been solved and the Derby site was turned over to almost 100 per cent Class 158 production, with on occasions upwards of 30 sets being under test or assembly.

The first sets off the production line were allocated to Scotland, followed by Yorkshire and the North East for TransPennine use, However, operational problems soon came to light, involving adhesion on steeply graded routes especially in the leaf fall season and braking problems with disk brakes. Major rectification programmes were put into force to rectify these issues, which slowed down the rate of delivery.

Although the main Class 158 build was for two-car sets, 17 units, designated for TransPennine use, were built as three-car units with a Motor Standard coupled between the two driving cars.

In the typical BR way, although the Class 158 fleet was deemed as 'standard', that was far from the case. The main power unit used for the fleet was the Cummins NT855R of 350hp, however to keep engine manufacture Perkins in the frame sets Nos 158815-862 were fitted with a Perkins 2006-TWH units of 350hp, while sets 158863-872, destined for the Welsh Marches route, were fitted with a higher output Cummins producing 400hp.

At the end of the Provincial sector Class 158 build, 10 two-car sets with all standard class seating and revised interiors were built for West Yorkshire PTE and originally painted in maroon and buttermilk colours.

By 1992 all sets were assembled and the production line turned to Class 159s for South West Trains. These were actually built as Class 158 body shells and then upgraded.

The Class 158 internal layout was set out in the 2+2 for standard class occupancy and 2+1 in first.

An interesting group of units were numbers 158747-751 which for a time were fitted with InterCity style interiors and used by Virgin Trains on the Manchester/Liverpool -

Below: *After many false starts the first complete (exterior wise) Class 158 No 158701 was shown to a small number of railway technical press at the Railway Technical Centre, Derby on 9 October 1989, when car No 57701 was rolled out. At this time the interior was far from complete and the vehicle was undergoing type test approval at the Engineering Development Unit. The car is carrying the then new 'Express' branding and this is one of the few pictures showing the unmodified support bracket between body and bogie, these were originally subject to cracking and all were modified with an indented centre to provide easy inspection.* **Author**

Above: *Most of the aluminium extrusions used in the fabrication of the Class 158s was sourced from Switzerland and delivered in huge strips and fabrication of floor, sides and roof sections, these were then formed together in a huge jig using sophisticated mobile aluminium welding technology. The body shell for car No 68, which eventually went into set No 158734 is seen in the main fabrication shop on 29 May 1990.* **Author**

Right: *In terms of works throughput, the Class 158 was a huge contract for BREL and most of the Derby Litchurch Lane plant was turned over to the production line. Viewed on 30 May 1990, car 52 is seen in the main construction bay. Its GRP yellow end has been fitted over the aluminium cab frame, windows have been fitted and interior wiring and underfloor equipment is being installed. When in full swing, a Class 158 was being turned out from sheet aluminium to operational train in around nine weeks.* **Author**

Edinburgh/Glasgow route until replaced by Voyager stock.

From the original build a number of major rebuilds and refurbishments have taken place. First Class has been added to sets at various times as dictated by the routes operated, while various seating styles have been used. Passenger access is by two pairs of double-leaf sliding plug doors on either side of each vehicle, feeding a cross-width walkway with sliding door access to the passenger saloons. The sets are corridor fitted throughout with a driving cab occupying one third of the outer end.

At the time of privatisation the Class 158 fleet could be found working throughout the Country and were well accepted by staff and passengers. The fleet today is owned by Porterbrook and Angel Trains and leased to

Arriva Trains Wales (24 x 2-car sets), East Midlands Trains (26 x 2-car sets), First Great Western (1 x 3-car and 20 2-car sets), First ScotRail (47 x 2-car sets), Northern Rail (8 x 3-car and 36 x 2-car sets) and South West Trains (9 x 2-car sets).

From the original Provincial Railways livery carried, a huge number of different colour schemes are now to be found, including advertising and pictogram brandings, some are route specific.

An interesting 'twist' to the Class 158 story came in 1991 when BREL won an export order for 20 Class 158 style vehicles for the State Railway of Thailand, who at the time were expanding their use of DMU-type trains onto longer-distance routes from Bangkok.

All 20 vehicles built were powered; 12 were cab cars with a driving cab at one end and

eight were intermediate cars, allowing formations of between 2 and 10 vehicles to operate.

The structural design, while based on the Class 158, incorporated metre-gauge bogies and deep step wells to facilitate access at low-level platforms.

Internally the sets were fitted with 2+2 leatherette-covered reclining seats, lino on the floors and Asian-style toilet compartments. The driving position was on the cabs right side and a small food preparation area was provided.

Numbered in the 25xx series the sets were finished in near exact Provincial Railways livery, complete with a yellow end. The cab ends differed slightly from the UK builds in not having a close coupled gangway, and had high-level headlights, a knuckle coupler and exterior mounted train supply and air pipes. ●

Above: *By August 1990 a number of complete Class 158s were parked up awaiting delivery at Derby Litchurch Lane while some rectification repairs were being arranged following operational experience with early sets. Nos 158734/729/733 are seen lined up in Litchurch Lane yard on 30 August 1990, awaiting final signing off and delivery to Haymarket, Scotland.* **Author**

Left: *The longer-distance regional services, such as the Nottingham to Cardiff service illustrated here were ideal for Class 158 deployment. Offering a comfortable 2+2 passenger environment, trolley catering service, air conditioning and good quality toilet facilities. Set No 158792 departs from Hillfield Tunnel and approaches Gaer Junction west of Newport on 2 April 1997.* **Author**

Left: *Another route which benefited largely from the introduction of Class 158s was the through service from Cardiff to Penzance, a route far too long in terms of mileage and travelling time for a standard DMU, but ideal for the 'Express' version. Branded with the later Regional Railways lettering, set No 158864, one of the Cummins 400hp (per vehicle) sets drops downgrade from Whiteball Tunnel towards Tiverton Parkway on 9 April 1997 forming the 11.55 Cardiff to Penzance semi-fast service. Sadly, with franchise changes no through service now exists between Cardiff and Penzance, passengers having to change trains in Bristol.* **Author**

Second Generation DMUs

Above: *Although installed with full air conditioning equipment, two staff-released hopper windows were provided on each side of both vehicles in case of system failures. In time this fitting was of a major benefit as numerous problems with air conditioning systems prevailed, either overheating interiors by blowing out hot air in the summer or by blowing out cold air in the winter. Major modifications were made to the heating systems and by 2009 the interior environment was much improved. Changes from the original CFC air conditioning to a more environmentally friendly gas was a directive of Government.* **Author**

Below: *The 17 original three-car Class 158s (158798-814) were built for the TransPennine route where passenger numbers dictated more than a two-car train. The intermediate Motor Standard (MS) was basically a driving car without a cab, it seated 70 standard class passengers in the 2+2 style and had one toilet compartment. The MS cars did not carry bodyside branding with their vehicle number carried at the right end. Set No 158806 stands at Middlesbrough on 31 July 1993 forming a Liverpool to Newcastle service.* **Author**

Above: *Numerically the final 10 Class 158s off the production line in Derby, Nos 158901-910 were built specifically for West Yorkshire PTE sponsored services, and were finished in their maroon and buttermilk livery. Destined for use on longer-distance Yorkshire services, the sets were allocated to Leeds Neville Hill. The interiors were slightly revised with only one toilet provided in the DMSL vehicle. On 25 June 2000, set No 158904 departs from Doncaster forming the 08.28 Cleethorpes to Manchester Airport service.* **Author**

Left: *Under privatisation until the end of 2007, the principal Midlands area operator was the aptly named Central Trains, who opted for a two tone green livery with cab end blue swirl as its livery. Looking rather garish compared to the original sedate colour scheme, set No 158860 departs from Derby on 16 May 2002 bound for Nottingham. By this time to meet the Disability Discrimination Act, the passenger doors had to carry a contrasting colour from the main body side to aid partly sighted people in finding the entrance to vehicles.* **Author**

Left: *Until 2006 changes in franchises and the formation of a much enlarged Great Western franchise, Arriva Trains Wales operated through services from Wales to the West Country, bringing a variety of different liveried units to Devon and Cornwall. In this 1 August 2004 view, an Arriva Trains-branded silver 'Alphaline' set No 158839 leads an Arriva turquoise liveried No 158818 through Aller west of Newton Abbot forming a Penzance to Cardiff duty. By the looks of the hopper windows being open, the air conditioning was not performing well on this train.* **Author**

Second Generation DMUs

Right: *Carrying Wessex Trains silver and pink 'Alphaline' colours set No 158870 stops at Par on 3 June 2005 while forming the 07.47 Penzance to Portsmouth Harbour train. This train was routed through Cornwall and then via Exeter and Taunton to Westbury where it changed direction to reach Salisbury, Southampton and the coastway route to Portsmouth Harbour. With franchise changes this is another through service which has been lost and passengers from the far west wanting to reach Portsmouth or the south coast towns have to either travel on South West Trains services via Salisbury to travel via London and return to the coast on a Southern train service.* **Author**

Right Middle: *With a very odd mix of Northern Spirit and First TransPennine livery one would hardly believe this picture was actually taken in Cornwall! The Class 158s operated by the Arriva Trains Northern (previously Northern Spirit) franchise and deployed on cross-Pennine services from Newcastle to Manchester and beyond, were transferred to the First TransPennine franchise when this was formed in February 2004. When Class 158s were displaced from the Pennine route by new Class 185s, the sets were sent south to First Great Western to assist with a power shortage. On 13 April 2007 set No 158761 passes Restormel near Lostwithiel forming the 12.42 Penzance to Plymouth service.* **Author**

Below: *Operating on its intended TransPennine route a three and two-car Class 158, led by set No 158812 await departure from York on 1 July 2004 bound for Manchester via Leeds. These services are now operated by Siemens Class 185 'Desiro' stock.* **Author**

Right: *A car park adjacent to the River Usk bridge between Newport station and Maindee West Junction provides an excellent photographic viewpoint of trains arriving and departing the station. On 1 March 1995, set No 158816 crosses the River Usk forming the 07.49 Milford Haven to Birmingham New Street service.* **Author**

Facing Page, Bottom Left and Right: *A large number of different interior layouts and seat styles have been fitted to the Class 158 design since original construction. These two views show the South West Trains treatment as applied to two sets in 2005 deployed on the Bristol Temple Meads - Salisbury - London Waterloo corridor. Subsequent stock changes have seen different units drafted into SWT service which have now all been refurbished with new-style seats in both classes.* **Author**

Below: *Following the franchise re-mapping which concentrated one principal rail operator for Welsh services, Arriva Trains Wales was awarded the franchise from 1 December 2003 and now trades as Arriva Trains Wales. Their distinctive turquoise livery is offset by cream doors which, while rather bright, does suit the body profile of the 158s. On 29 June 2007, set No 158818 departs from Newport forming the 11.17 Maesteg to Gloucester service.* **Author**

Above: *One of the smartest of the privatised rail operator liveries has to be that of South West Trains, a Stagecoach company, who although using white as a predominant colour manage to keep their trains clean. No 158786, a set only operated by SWT for a short time in 2005-06, is seen at Bristol Temple Meads on 6 July 2005 for the launch of the SWT through service between Bristol Temple Mead and London Waterloo.* **Author**

Below: *Following the successful development of vinyl vehicle branding, the rail industry has been involved in a number of full train advertising deals, where a business will fund the complete re-livery of a train in their house colours for a limited period. One of the first was Ginsters, the Cornish pasty maker, who funded full train branding in 2003-05. Set No 158827 in Ginsters livery and No 158845 in Central Trains colours depart from Dawlish on 3 July 2004 with the daily Manchester to Penzance semi-fast service.* **Author**

Second Generation DMUs

Above: *During the period of the Wessex Trains franchise the South West operator took the application of bodyside pictograms one stage further, using the technology for route and line advertising and forming a number of bonds with the local community, such as the special 'Alphaline' style branding incorporating local pictures of the Exmoor area. The set was officially named* Exmoor *in an event on the privately owned West Somerset Railway at Minehead on 19 May 2004. The immaculate set is seen approaching Blue Anchor while returning to the National Network at Norton Fitzwarren.* **Author**

Below: *Following stock changes in late 2007, First Great Western became the operator of just one three-car Class 158, which is scheduled to operate on commuter flows in the Bristol area where huge overcrowding problems prevailed following service changes in 2007. In early 2008 the set, No 158798, was fully refurbished at Wabtec Doncaster and is seen on 9 February 2008 at Cardiff Central.* **Stacey Thew**

Above: *During the course of Class 158 body shell production a couple of extra shells were produced. One was used as a replacement for an accident damaged vehicle in set No 158861, while another was used for crash testing at Litchurch Lane Works. The vehicle in raw aluminium was glazed and fitted with some seating and weight block and some of its underframe equipment. The cab end was finished with a half height centre glazed door. The vehicle was given the number of 158999 and survived around the works usually out of public view until late 1993. This view was taken on 11 March 1993 soon after a mock collision with a Mk1 coach was carried out.* **Author**

Left: *One of the few accidents to befall the Class 158s was on 25 March 1994 when set No 158833 forming the 09.40 Paignton to Cardiff collided at relatively slow speed with HST powercar No 43071 at Newton Abbot. The HST was waiting to depart on the 07.20 Penzance to Edinburgh when the Class 158 approached the station having failed to stop at the protecting signal. The driver of the 158 saw the HST ahead of him as he rounded the curve into the station, but even a full emergency brake application failed to prevent a collision. Taken about 45 minutes after the accident, this view shows the result.* **Author**

Left: *The Class 158 driving cab was based on the previous second generation DMU designs. The power or throttle control is operated by the driver's right hand, while the brake valve is worked by the driver's left hand. The angled display panel has just two gauges for speed and brake pressure. All desk-mounted switches are of the 'press and illuminate' type. The switch gear on the left of the brake gauge operates the head, marker and tail lights. On the right bulkhead wall the cab radio can be seen, while the isolation switches for the AWS and the emergency by-pass switch are on the flat of the window ledge. The AWS 'sunflower' is seen upper left, while passenger door release buttons are on the front edge of the desk.* **Author**

Above: *In 1990 mid-way through the UK Class 158 order came the news that BREL had been awarded the contract to build 20 similar vehicles for The State Railways of Thailand. The coach bodies, 22.16m long and 2.8m wide, were assembled on the Class 158 production line and were finished in a very similar livery to the BR Provincial sector. The body shell for the first driving car No 2501 is seen on works stands during the early fitting out stage.* **Author**

Right: *One of the most significant changes on the Thailand vehicles was in the passenger and staff access. The exterior doors were of the single leaf slam type. While the cars were fitted with high-output air conditioning each window was equipped with an opening hopper. Apparently standing on standard gauge track in the test house at Derby Litchurch Lane on 22 March 1991 is driving car No 2504.* **Author**

Right: *The interior of the Thailand sets was a far cry from the plush interior of the UK Class 158s, with leatherette seats finished in red and grey, a lino-covered floor and spartan interior decor. As the sets were scheduled to operate long-distance routes, manually-operated pull-down window blinds were fitted to each window. The interior of vehicle 2501 is illustrated, looking away from the driving cab end.* **Author**

Second Generation DMUs

Following the formation of Network SouthEast and announcements of major investment to improve the business sector's rail network, came the agreement to modernise the Waterloo-Salisbury-Exeter line. The line was currently operated by a mix of Class 33s, 47s and 50s using Mk2 passenger stock, which was getting old and the traction unreliable. Various options for modernisation were considered, from replacement loco-hauled stock and refurbished diesels to a radical upgrade to purpose-built DMUs.

Eventually during the Class 158 build programme, NSE submitted plans for a batch of 22 three-car Class 158 style sets to be added on the end of the Class 158 build. The units would be fabricated at BREL Derby and built to an operational condition, and would then be transferred to Babcock Rail at Rosyth Dockyard for upgrade to NSE requirements - the result was one of the best DMU trains ever built.

The fleet of 22 units, allocated the number range 159001-159022 were built in 1992-93 and finished in full NSE livery, the units were then driven to Rosyth Dockyard under their own power and totally rebuilt internally. A half-vehicle-length first class area using 2+1 seating was put in one driving car, while standard class seating was in the 2+2 style. Improved seating, carpets and interior furniture from that used on the Class 158s made these sets quieter and more comfortable.

New purpose-built depot facilities were constructed at Salisbury and the line was operated on an out and back basis with each set receiving maintenance daily at the high-quality facility.

When introduced in early 1993 the 159s revolutionised rail travel on the Waterloo-Exeter route and also provided a limited through service to Paignton and Plymouth.

The Class 159s were installed with the higher-output 400hp engine per vehicle.

The 22 sets passed to Stagecoach South West Trains in 1996 and have always remained on their intended route. With service developments, especially following the re-awarding of the SWT franchise to Stagecoach in 2006, extra trains were sought and the answer was found in a batch of eight three-car Class 158s which had become spare following introduction of Class 185s on the First TransPennine route. The 'new' three-car sets were fully refurbished to a very high standard at Wabtec Doncaster and reclassified Class 159/1 (Nos 159101-159108); these sets are, however, fitted with lower-output 350hp engines.

The interior of these Wabtec refurbishments brought new levels of interior decor and ambience to SWT travel and following the introduction of the Class 159/1 fleet, a full refurbishment of the existing Class 159/0 fleet was authorised including CCTV, power points and a passenger information system.

When built sets were finished in standard Network SouthEast colours; this incorporated Stagecoach branding after 1996 and today full South West Trains white, red and blue colours are carried. ●

Below: *Clearly based on the Class 158 concept, this drawing was issued of the proposed West of England stock replacement in late 1999, showing a rather pleasing all-grey front end, with just a yellow 'bib' around the coupling pocket.* **Author's Collection**

Above: *After building and final testing at BREL Derby Litchurch Lane, all 22 Class 159s were taken under their own power to Babcock Rail's small engineering facility in the centre of Rosyth Dockyard. Here very basic depot facilities existed with the interior upgrade carried out in two drive-through sheds and one small workshop. Some interior fittings were installed at Derby, but the seating and interior trim was added at Rosyth. It was usual for three sets to be on site at one time for upgrade work. This was the view on 6 January 1993 with sets Nos 159004, 159008 and 159006 receiving attention.* **Author**

Below: *Once in traffic on the Waterloo-Salisbury-Exeter route, the sets worked alongside the loco-hauled operation for just a short period before full deployment, offering a much enhanced service on the route. Sadly little improvement could be made west of Yeovil Junction due to the predominance of the single-track railway. Carrying 'as delivered' NSE livery, sets Nos 159010 and 159013 pass Surbiton on the down fast line on 10 July 1996 forming the 16.35 Waterloo to Exeter service. When in normal use, the first class driving car is usually formed at the London end of trains.* **Author**

Above: *Shown on paperwork of the day as receiving 'modification' work, driving car 52883 from set 159011 stands on supports inside the main fitting-out shop at by then the ABB Works in Derby, ABB having taken over from BREL during the course of the build. On the left is a Metropolitan Line London Underground set receiving refurbishment.* **Author**

Below: *After privatisation Stagecoach South West Trains soon applied their distinctive livery to sets, using the main line white scheme, offset by swirl ends of orange and red with a blue solebar band. On 1 June 2005, set No 159013 passes Powderham forming the 07.10 Waterloo to Paignton through service.* **Author**

Second Generation DMUs

Above: *Each day several of the Waterloo-Salisbury-Exeter services are extended to either Paignton or Plymouth providing a welcome alternative service to that provided by the principal operator First Great Western. In the main these SWT services call at all stations west of Exeter. On 2 July 2005 sets Nos 159003 and 159004 pass along the Dawlish Sea Wall at Rockstone Bridge forming the 10.09 Paignton to Portsmouth Harbour service.* **Author**

Right: *Taken through a powerful telephoto lens, this is the view of a pair of Class 159/0s Nos 159008 and 159009 approaching Byfleet & New Haw station with the 10.20 London Waterloo to Exeter St Davids service on 27 October 2006. In the far distance Weybridge station can be seen, while the 30mph speed restriction board on the left is for diverging trains taking the line to Chertsey and Staines.* **Chris Nevard**

Right: *With the average two-hourly service from London Waterloo to Exeter St Davids, plus Salisbury and Yeovil terminators, Class 159s are seen on the main line between Waterloo and Salisbury on average twice per hour. With an apparent full house at Surbiton on 10 July 2007, No 159020 traverses the up main with the 09.45 Salisbury to Waterloo, while a Desiro Class 450 heads south on the down slow line and a Desiro Class 444 passes on the down main. On the far right a Class 455 slows for the station stop with a Hampton Court to Waterloo service.* **Author**

Above: *Rounding off the Plymouth main line at Aller, Newton Abbot on 1 August 2004, a six-car formation made up of units Nos 159019 and 159022 heads towards Exeter and Waterloo via Salisbury with the 14.16 Penzance to Waterloo train. In 2003 South West Trains introduced one through service to Penzance each week, working west on a Saturday and returning on a Sunday. Problems with FGW staff in Cornwall not being trained on Class 159s has always plagued the service and frequently the services terminate at Plymouth.* **Author**

Left: *A couple of miles south of Basingstoke lies Worting Junction, where the lines to Winchester and Salisbury diverge. The main electrified line continues through Winchester, Southampton and onto Bournemouth and Weymouth, while the Salisbury and Exeter non-electrified line veers right. Heading west on the down main line, Class 159 No 159019 prepares to swing onto the Andover line on 25 August 2006 while forming the 13.20 Waterloo to Yeovil Junction service.* **Chris Perkins**

Above: *The high-quality Class 159/1 conversions from three-car Class 158s started to enter service in December 2006 and immediately brought new standards of comfort to SWT passengers. On 23 March 2007 sets Nos 159105 and 159014 arrive at Salisbury with the 07.50 service from London Waterloo.* **Author**

Right: *First class interior of Class 159/1, showing the plush new reclining seats with hinged armrests, a door divider between the first and standard class, tables and above-seat spot lighting. Since this view was taken CCTV equipment has also been installed.* **Author**

Below: *The eight members of the Class 159/1 fleet operate in one pool with the Class 159/0s and can be found anywhere on the SWT diesel network. On 5 April 2007, set No 159108 rounds the curve at Langstone Rock, Dawlish forming the 07.10 Waterloo to Paignton service.* **Author**

Soon after the formation of Network SouthEast under the leadership of Managing Director Chris Green came the announcement that new multiple unit rolling stock was to be ordered for both the Chiltern routes from London Marylebone and the Thames routes from London Paddington..

A new design of 'standard' rolling stock was to be ordered using the 'Networker' fleet name, with both diesel and electric versions planned.

In terms of the diesel variant, the design was deemed as the 'Networker Turbo' with an order for 180 vehicles placed with ABB for construction at their York Works.

The order was split between Chiltern and Thames, with both having a mix of two- and three-car sets. Chiltern sets were classified as 165/0 and Thames sets as 165/1. As built the units looked identical, except that Chiltern sets had a top speed of 75mph and were fitted with LUL style tripcock equipment, while Thames sets had a top speed of 90mph.

The first sets off the production line were 28 two-car sets (DMCL+DMS) for Chiltern numbered 165001-165028, followed by 11 three-car sets (DMCL+MS+DMS) Nos 165029-165039. The design incorporated a full-width driving cab and no end gangway connections. Passenger accommodation was in the high-density 2+2 for first and 2+3 for standard class passengers. Door positions were at the one and two-third positions and used a sliding plug design. One toilet was provided in the DMCL coach. The total seating on a two-car set was for 170 standard and 16 first, while a three-car unit accommodated 276 standard and 16 first.

The first complete set was handed over at York Works on 15 February 1991 when the BRB Chairman Sir Bob Reid and NSE Managing Director Chris Green took delivery of set No 165001.

The Thames sub-sector sets were the next off the York production line, classified 165/1 and numbered 165101-117 for three-car sets and 165118-137 for two-car sets. Due to the area

of use NSE stipulated extra first class accommodation on these sets and thus the seating was 24 first and 158 standard on a two-car set and 24 first and 264 standard on a three-car set.

On Chiltern the units were allocated to new purpose-built depot facilities at Aylesbury, while Thames sets were looked after at upgraded facilities at Reading depot. On the Chiltern routes the new sets replaced the Class 115s, while on Thames an ageing fleet of Heritage sets were replaced from the inner-suburban routes.

These sets were unique in a number of ways; they were the first production passenger fleet of DMUs to use aluminium construction and were the first to be delivered incorporating full automatic train protection. Two different systems were used as the Chilterns and Western Region lines were trial fittings of different systems.

Under privatisation the sets remained on their intended routes working for new

Below: *Following the official handover of the first Class 165 at York Works to NSE on 15 February 1991 considerable static and dynamic testing was carried out before the first two sets were transferred to Aylesbury depot, where a special media event to publicise the modernisation of the Chiltern route was held on 14 May 1991 when sets Nos 165001 and 165002 were positioned outside the depot for photography. Fitted with BSI couplers, these sets are only able to intercouple with Class 166 and 168 units.* **Author**

operators. Much refurbishing was done and this included installing air cooling on the Chiltern fleet (a form of low-cost air conditioning) which allowed the opening hopper windows to be removed. Chiltern sets also lost their first class seating. Sets operated by Thames passed to Go-Ahead in 1996 and later FirstGroup, a number of refinements being made and different liveries carried.

At the time of privatisation a handful of the Chiltern designed Class 165/0s were working on the Thames routes, these were later transferred to their intended line when Class 180s were introduced.

Originally sets were painted in NSE livery, this gave way to Thames and Chiltern colours with the First Great Western sets now sporting FGW 'dynamic lines' colours.

One set has been withdrawn, No 165115 which was involved in the Ladbroke Grove accident on 5 October 1999. ●

Above Right: *Both the diesel and electric versions of the Networker used welded aluminium for the fabrication of the body shells. This was undertaken in special facilities at York works using imported aluminium from Switzerland formed as side, roof and floor sections and then married together in a 'Minster Jig'. In this view one of the cars for set No 165003 is seen on the right, with its pre-formed cab section already mounted on the body structure, while on the left a near-complete bodyshell for a Class 465 EMU is seen.* **Author**

Right Bottom: *By 1994 the vast majority of local services working from Paddington to Oxford, Bedwyn and the London branches were in the hands of Class 165s. Looking in immaculate condition, NSE-liveried set No 165120 approaches Acton Main Line on 24 June 1994 forming the 12.55 Paddington to Greenford all stations service. On the left a rake of Bardon hoppers climbs the bank from Acton Yard to Willesden.* **Author**

Above: *The Chiltern-operated Class 165/0s received major refurbishment following privatisation, with significant changes to interiors, fitting of an air cooling system which allowed the previous opening hopper windows to be removed and the fitting of a revised front end light cluster to smooth off the appearance of the cab ends. Painted in standard Chiltern blue and white livery with reverse colouring on the passenger doors to meet the Disability Discrimination Act, set No 165031 is seen at Quainton Road working a Betjeman charter on 2 September 2006.* **Author**

Below: *Chiltern also operate a major maintenance facility at Wembley North London, which shares maintenance of the Class 165s and 168 stock. As well as Aylesbury, stabling of sets is also to be found at London Marylebone, where this view of set No 165033 was taken on 2 September 2006.* **Author**

Above: Under the Go-Ahead operation of the Thames franchise a revised livery of white and blue was introduced with the suburban sets having a stylised 'O' applied in green over the door positions. This livery remained after the FirstGroup take-over of operations, which saw First branding applied. The livery remained until 2007 when standard FirstGroup Dynamic Lines colours were applied. Set No 165103 pulls into Reading station on 8 January 2007 with an Oxford to Paddington semi-fast service. **Author**

Right: In support of London's 2012 Olympic Games bid a number of trains were adorned in 'Support the Bid' mid-blue livery in February 2005, one set selected was Class 165 No 165136, illustrated departing from one of the bay platforms at Reading bound for Basingstoke on 8 January 2007. **Author**

Right : All the FGW Class 165s are allocated to Reading depot, and thus the area around Reading is a stronghold to view and photograph the class. The new FGW Dynamic Lines colours look excellent in night photography, especially these days when white balance can be re-calibrated for exposures to ensure the correct colour tones are recorded. Three-car set No 165111 is seen at Reading at 05.14 on the morning of 16 February 2008 after arriving empty stock from the nearby depot. **Stacey Thew**

Following the order for two and three-car Class 165 units for use on Chiltern and Thames line services came a follow-on order for 21 three-car sets for outer-suburban or main line use for deployment on the Thames routes working from Paddington to Oxford and onto Worcester as well as on the Reading-Gatwick 'North Downs' line.

These sets followed the same structural design as the Class 165 units, again being built at York and originally finished in Network SouthEast livery.

Delivered in 1993, the units incorporated full air conditioning and thus did not incorporate any opening hopper windows. To provide a passenger service a catering point was provided for a trolley.

Passenger areas were all carpeted, with first class using the 2+2 layout and standard class the 2+3 style; in total accommodation was provided for 32 first class and 243 standard class passengers.

Technically the trains were the same as the Class 165 three-car units. Allocation of sets was to Reading depot.

After delivery and staff training at Reading, the first sets entered service from 11 May 1993, when a set operated a special press and user groups preview run from London Paddington (departing at 10.20) to Oxford; in Oxford guests were transported to a local hotel for a full update on Thames operations and the introduction of the new stock.

Under privatisation the sets became the property of Angel Trains. Repainting from NSE colours to Thames (Go-Ahead) livery of white and mid-blue was done during overhauls at Ilford depot and saw the same

basic colour as applied to the Thames Class 165s used; however, on these main-line sets a stylised 'S' was applied in apple green over the door positions.

After a few years Go-Ahead surrendered the franchise to FirstGroup, which operated the London area lines as First Great Western Link. Upon the April 2004 re-mapping of rail franchises, the former Thames routes were taken over fully by FirstGroup and are now operated as part of the First Great Western franchise, with sets repainted into FGW Dynamic Lines livery.

Seating has remained largely the same since construction; by 2009 standard class will have been reduced to 227 standard class passengers per three-car set, while first class remains the same with 16 seated in each driving car. ●

Above and Left: *In immaculate condition, set No 166202 stands at Oxford on 11 May 1993 awaiting departure back to London after operating the fleet launch special from Paddington. The Class 166s were welcomed into traffic by the then Transport Secretary Roger Freeman. If these two views are compared with the Class 165s (in as built condition) the omission of some opening hopper windows provides recognition between the two Networker Turbo types. The Class 166s were officially known as Networker Turbo Express, a name which was soon dropped. Note that no NSE branding is carried by the intermediate coach apart from the running number.*
Both: **Author**

Above: *Photographed in one of the aluminium assembly shops at ABB York Works on 9 December 1992, the day the final Class 165 departed from the works. One of the driving cars for the third Class 166 No 166203 is all but formed and awaits floor pan drilling, insertion of window frames and mid-dividers. All the aluminium for the Class 166s was supplied from Switzerland and then cut and formed into shape in York.* **Author**

Above & Right: *Class 166 interior. In first class (shown above), 16 seats were provided directly behind the driving cab in both driving cars, occupying the space as far as the first door position. Seats were in facing pairs with a good size table. Non-hinged armrests were provided, making access to the window seats a little difficult. Standard class seating (shown right) was in the 2+2 and 2+3 style and used medium-height seats, in a mix of airline and groups. Several tables were provided throughout the train, especially useful on longer journeys. Above seat luggage racks were fitted throughout and grab handles provided on seat backs. Standard class seating was originally covered in mid-blue moquette. Edward Pond murals of Thames area subjects were located on end bulkhead walls. Both:* **Author**

Above and Inset: *In August 2000 a start was made to replace the Network South East livery on the Thames operated Class 165 and 166 fleet, as part of a mini-refurbishment carried out at the then Adtranz-controlled site at Ilford. The first set to be overhauled and repainted into Thames Trains Express livery of blue and white with a green stylised 'S' over the doors was set No 166221, photographed at Ilford on 16 August 2000. The inset image shows the intermediate MS coach with Thames Trains Express branding. Both:* **Author**

Right: *When first introduced, the NSE Class 166s operated north of Oxford to Worcester. With the line north of Oxford technically operated by Regional Railways, the Turbo Express fleet was operated under a joint NSE/Regional Railways banner over this section. On 20 July 2000, set No 166204 arrives at Moreton-in-Marsh, pulling off the single line section from Norton Junction, forming the 15.53 Great Malvern to London Paddington.* **Author**

Second Generation DMUs

Above: *At the end of 2006, First Great Western, which amalgamated the Thames, Great Western and Wessex franchises from 1 April 2006, finalised a new livery for all its rolling stock, based on the standard FirstGroup 'Dynamic Lines' branding applied over FirstGroup blue. Set No 166215 shows this livery at Reading on 7 January 2007, forming an Oxford to Paddington semi-fast service.* **Author**

Below: *The present North Downs service from Reading to Gatwick Airport via Redhill is the modern day operation of the BR Southern Region Reading to Tonbridge service which operated with the unique 3-car 'Tadpole' units. The present FGW service uses Class 165 or 166 sets on an out-and-back duty from Reading. On 27 October 2007 the 11.01 FGW service from Reading to Gatwick Airport, formed of set No 166210, approaches its destination.* **Brian Morrison**

18 Class 168

After the privatisation of the UK rail industry in the mid-1990s and the formation slightly earlier of rolling stock lease companies, no new train orders were placed for a lengthy period. During this time most of the main manufacturers were hard at work refining train designs perceived for future ordering.

Adtranz, now Bombardier, produced the plans for its Turbostar range, a modular design of multiple unit which was offered with electric propulsion (Electrostar) or diesel propulsion (Turbostar).

Porterbrook Leasing was the first company to close negotiations with Adtranz for a small fleet of Turbostar products for lease to newly-formed Chiltern Railways, which was in need of extra rolling stock for its London Marylebone to Birmingham service.

The order for five sets was fulfilled at the Litchurch Lane plant in Derby and was the forerunner to the highly successful Class 170

Turbostar product.

The Chiltern Class 168s, or Clubman trains as the operators chose to call them, were well received by passengers and soon growth on the route required extra trains. At first additional non-driving Motor Standards were ordered and eventually in small orders the fleet has grown to 19 sets by 2008. A mix of three and four-car formations are operated, with sets based at Aylesbury.

The first five sets are to the earlier body profile with a rather ugly front end design, while all follow on orders have used the standard Class 170 style body profile. Some detail differences do exist on production sets with light-group designs on the front ends which were standardised during the course of assembly.

The vehicles are formed of welded aluminium extrusions onto which a cab module is 'bolted'. The interior layout uses 2+2 seating throughout, with bi-parting

sliding plug doors at the one and two third positions, a separate sliding plug door is provided for access into the driving cab.

The cab is of full width design, with standard Turbostar cab controls. All vehicles are powered using an underfloor mounted MTU 6R183TD13H power unit set to deliver 422hp. This drives a Voith hydraulic transmission. The sets top speed is 100mph and Chiltern Line Automatic Train Protection (ATP) is fitted.

As the units operate over the London Underground Metropolitan Line, LU style 'trip cocks' are fitted to bogies. This system applies the train's brakes if an LU signal is passed at danger.

All sets are painted in Chiltern Railways white and blue livery, with passenger doors in a contrasting shade of the same colours.

It is not expected that any further Class 168s will be built. In early 2008 Chiltern opted to order Class 172 stock. ●

Below: *The first of the privatised railways' new passenger trains, the Class 168 was shown off to the rail and trade media in a special event at the then Adtranz plant at Derby Litchurch Lane on 19 November 1997, when what was in fact the first of the 'Turbostar' product range was unveiled. With the front end developed from the Network Turbo, one of the driving cars for the first set, No 168001, is seen inside the works test hall. After the first five sets were built, Adtranz refined the 'Turbostar' product with a more pleasing front end. Since this photograph was taken, to meet the Disability Discrimination Act the passenger doors have been re-branded in reverse contrasting colours.* **Author**

Second Generation DMUs

Right: *When first introduced, soon after the privatisation of the UK railways in the mid-1990s, the 'Clubman' Class 168 units were allocated to Aylesbury depot and shared space with Class 165s. This facility was clearly not able to offer the level of maintenance sought by operators Chiltern and new and expanded maintenance facilities were sought. This came in 2005 when a new depot was commissioned at Wembley, where a small shed building and stabling sidings are provided. Chiltern Railways Class 168 'Clubman' No 168002 is seen stabled inside Wembley depot on 7 September 2005.*
Brian Morrison

Below: *Formed of one of the original Class 168/0 sets, No 168002, the 16.10 Chiltern service from Birmingham Snow Hill to London Marylebone makes its scheduled stop at Leamington Spa on 12 May 2006. Since introduction a number of reformations have taken place with several small orders placed for extra vehicles as line growth demanded. The Class 168/0 sets, although with a slightly different front end, are all technically part of the Adtranz/Bombardier 'Turbostar' product range.*
Brian Morrison

Above: *After the first tranche of Class 168s were constructed the 'standard' Class 170 style front end was adopted for the entire range of non-corridor fitted Turbostars. Three-car set No 168113 is recorded passing Tyseley on 15 March 2006, forming a Chiltern service from Birmingham Snow Hill to London Marylebone.* **Brian Morrison**

Below: *Even during the course of construction of the standard body profile Class 168s, further changes were made to the headlight and marker/tail light groups, with replacement of the three individual lights on each side by one cluster. With the revised front end, set No 168214 arrives at Princes Risborough on 16 June 2005.* **Nathan Williamson**

Second Generation DMUs

Above: *One of the earlier three-car sets, No 168108 forms the 13.27 Princes Risborough to London Marylebone through Beaconsfield on 2 April 2006. The formation of the Chiltern sets, sees two members of Class 168/1 operating as four-car sets and six operating as three-car formations. A similar split exists within the Class 168/2 sub-class with three sets formed as three-car and three sets as four-car units.* **Ken Brunt**

Below: *Due to passenger loading, some of the peak hour services on the London Marylebone to Birmingham corridor are formed of two unit consists. On 8 September 2006, set No 168112 leads another three-car set past a public crossing just north of King's Sutton station in gorgeous evening light heading for Britain's second city.* **Chris Nevard**

Above: *One of the later-built Class 168/2 sets, No 168215, having an identical body profile to a Class 17x Turbostar, passes King's Sutton on 8 September 2006 forming the 17.00 London Marylebone to Kidderminster service. The success of the Chiltern operation, providing an attractive alternative to Virgin Trains for London to Birmingham passengers, has led to continued growth with several 'follow-on' stock orders placed.* **Mark Bearton**

Left: *The Adtranz/Bombardier plant at Litchurch Lane, Derby has been responsible for the entire build of Class 168 vehicles. In this view Motor Second No 58460 is seen in the main test area on 16 May 2002. This vehicle is currently operating within set No 168110.* **Author**

Second Generation DMUs

Top Right: *The one class 'Clubman' interior of the Class 168 is set out in low-density 2+2 mode, with a mix of airline and group configuration. In comfort and space terms the seating is mid-way between standard and first class quality.* **Author**

Above Right: *The Chiltern route demonstrates the evolution of modern DMU design, with examples of the BREL/NSE Class 168s and the two styles of the next generation of medium distance multiple unit designs working alongside each other. In this view at Marylebone, Class 168 No 168111 shares platform space with Class 165 No 165020.* **Author**

Right: *As the Class 168 sets operate over shared London Underground Metropolitan Line tracks in the London area, the fleet is equipped with 'trip cocks'; these are attached to the bogie on a trip-cock beam.* **Nathan Williamson**

Following Adtranz's success with the 'Clubman' Class 168 design for Chiltern Railways, the Turbostar product was born. Shortly after privatisation, many of the franchise holders were seeking new trains for medium- and longer-distance use and the Adtranz Turbostar product, now offered in a slightly refined form with a new cab design, was the obvious choice, The fleet had UK type test approval so could be built quickly and go straight into traffic.

From 1998 much of the workshop space at Derby Litchurch Lane was handed over to the Turbostar production line, using welded aluminium technology derived from the Class 158 build a few years prior.

The first train operator to opt for the Turbostar was Midland Mainline, which through Porterbrook Leasing procured a fleet of 17 two-car Class 170/1 sets; 10 sets were later augmented to three-car formation. After a period these sets were replaced and worked for Central Trains and now work for CrossCountry.

ScotRail (now First ScotRail), the largest user of the design with a fleet of 59 three-car sets, took delivery of their trains between 1999 and 2005. Different interiors on some sets, with all standard class seating, are dedicated to the Glasgow commuter belt. The then Central Trains operation took delivery of 33 sets in 1999-2000 formed as either two-car (Class 170/5) or three-car (Class 170/6) for Midlands area operations. These sets are now split between the Cross Country and London Midland franchises.

The Anglia route, now National Express Anglia operate the 170/2 sub-class; eight units are formed of three cars and four are two-car sets.

South West Trains originally operated a fleet of eight sets to augment the Class 159s on diesel routes, but following additional Class 158s and 159s being made available the units are now operated by First TransPennine Express.

A small batch of seven sets was built for Porterbrook and used for spot or short-term hire, four sets originally working with Hull Trains, but today these sets are operated by First TransPennine, First ScotRail and London Midland.

Being a modular train, numerous interior designs have been carried, using 2+2 for standard class seating and in the main 2+1 for first class. Some units for longer-distance work were equipped with buffet facilities when built but these have now been removed to satisfy traffic growth.

All sets are built to a common structural design, with two pairs of bi-parting sliding plug doors on each side of each vehicle. A separate sliding plug door is provided for the cab. Passenger doors feed a transverse walkway from where bi-parting doors lead into the passenger saloons. Full air conditioning is provided as is a passenger information system. All Turbostar vehicles are powered by a MTU 6R 183TD underfloor engine driving a Voith final drive unit. The maximum speed of units is 100mph and all are fitted with BSI autocouplers. ●

Below: *One of the Anglia Railways Class 170/2 two-car sets, No 170272, is seen in the main assembly shop at Bombardier Derby Litchurch Lane on 16 May 2002. The modular construction of the vehicle is quite apparent from this view, which shows the cab end, the assembly of which will be bolted on the end of the floor, side and roof members. As will be seen the body sides are pre-painted. On the right are a pair of side body sections for a Chiltern Railways Class 168 intermediate vehicle.* **Author**

Above: *The near-clinical assembly conditions in the Litchurch Lane facility of Bombardier Transportation are a world away from the old oily workshop conditions of just a few years ago. One of the driving cars for Anglia set No 170201 receives attention to its coupling before being bogied and commencing static tests on 16 May 2002.* **Author**

Below: *Originally the ScotRail Class 170/4 fleet were finished in a white, mauve, green and orange livery as shown on set No 170411 approaching Montrose on 12 August 2003, forming an Edinburgh Waverley to Aberdeen semi-fast service. All of the original ScotRail sets had first class accommodation located in both driving cars directly behind the driving position.* **Author**

Above: *The first operator of Class 170 'Turbostar' sets in passenger service was Midland Mainline, with their two-car sets classified as 170/1, allocated to Derby Etches Park and used on semi-fast services on the Derby and Nottingham to St Pancras service. Traffic growth on the route eventually led to some sets being augmented to three-car formation before eventual replacement with longer Class 222 sets. On 7 September 1999, sets Nos 170105 and 170109 approach Loughborough forming the 11.56 Nottingham to St Pancras.* **Author**

Below: *South West Trains, owned by Stagecoach, took the lease of eight Porterbrook Class 170/3s from November 2000 to supplement its fleet of Class 159s, with increased work on the Waterloo to Exeter line plus Reading to Brighton services. Allocated to Salisbury alongside the Class 159s, the 170s were used on the Waterloo-Yeovil and Reading-Brighton route as well as the Romsey-Southampton service. The fleet was replaced with a 'new' batch of Class 159/1s in 2006-07 and the 170/3s are now refurbished and operate for First TransPennine Express. Sets Nos 170308 and 170303 are seen inside Salisbury depot.* **Author**

Above: *The original three-car Anglia sets, which were delivered to operate on routes such as the Colchester-Woking cross-London service were quickly repainted into 'one' livery following franchise changes. The sets operate on the non-electrified branch lines as well as the London Liverpool Street to Peterborough routes. On 28 November 2006, set No 170208, painted in the rather gaudy 'one' livery, is seen at Ipswich, forming a Peterborough to Liverpool Street semi-fast service.* **Author**

Middle: *First ScotRail-operated sets numbered above 170450 are designed for all-standard class occupancy and are usually used on the Glasgow/Edinburgh outer suburban routes. Set No 170458 runs off the Forth Bridge at Dalmeny on 1 October 2005 leading a Class 158 unit forming a Fife Circle service.* **Chris Perkins**

Right: *Painted in Strathclyde PTE carmine and cream livery, one of the PTE-funded sets, No 170476 passes Greenhill Lower junction on 23 March 2005 forming a Glasgow Queen Street to Stirling service.* **Chris Perkins**

Above: *Birmingham-based Central Trains took delivery of two batches of Turbostars in 1999-2000, 23 sets were two-car formation and 10 were three-car. From delivery the sets were finished in two-tone green off-set by yellow passenger doors and a blue swirl at the cab ends. Sporting the Central Trains website address on the bodyside, set No 170511 stops at Newport (Gwent) forming the 07.00 Nottingham to Cardiff service on 29 June 2007.* **Author**

Middle: *Each of the Central Trains 2-car sets accommodated 122 standard class passengers while the strengthened three-car sets seated 196. Today, with franchise changes introduced at the end of 2007, the ex-Central sets are allocated to Cross Country and London Midland. These changes were to be reflected in new liveries and major interior refurbishment. Set No 170518 passes Stenson Junction on 23 April 2004 forming a Derby to Birmingham service.* **Author**

Left: *For many years the Porterbrook 'spot hire' Turbostar sets were painted in a base white livery with purple passenger doors. Depending on who the hirer was various brandings were applied. Here set No 170397 departs from Birmingham New Street branded with Central Trains markings.* **Author**

Second Generation DMUs

Above: *Still painted in the distinctive Anglia turquoise and white livery, two-car set No 170273 departs from Norwich on 22 November 2007. Fitted with a mix of first and standard class accommodation these twin sets seat nine first and 110 standard class passengers and offer a high-quality travelling environment for rural services in Norfolk. These sets are scheduled to be repainted in the revised National Express East Anglia livery in the near future.* **Author**

Below: *The application of the new Arriva CrossCountry franchise started to appear on the Class 170 fleet from mid-February 2008, with sets being dealt with by the EWS paint shops at Toton and Marcroft. On 22 February 2008, set No 170116 approaches Derby with the 13.13 Birmingham to Nottingham service. Initially the interiors were not 'refreshed' but a major upgrade was planned at the time of writing.* **John Binch**

ADtranz Turbostar - Traveller

On 21 November 2000, Adtranz unveiled a demonstration vehicle at Railtex 2000 called the Turbostar Traveller, based on a standard Turbostar vehicle. The project was aimed at providing operators of urban and rural routes with a slightly lower-cost alternative. The plan was to use a MAN 338kW engine under each vehicle giving a top speed of 120km/h.

The interiors were finished to a slightly lower specification than the production Class 170 and used a 2+2 seating configuration; however, the interior could be tailored to any operators specific needs.

Although the Traveller used one driving car of set No 170399 no takers came forward and the project was abandoned after the takeover by Bombardier Transportation.

Below: *The 'Turbostar Traveller' stands in the exhibition hall at the NEC, Birmingham during Railtex 2000.* **Author**

Right: *The intermediate non-driving vehicles for Class 170 Turbostar stock first emerged with the delivery of the ScotRail sets. After this additional intermediate cars were built for insertion into 10 Midland Main Line units, Middle cars were also provided for Class 170/3 'Spot hire' units, 170/2s for Anglia and 10 of the Central Trains batch. On the Midland and Anglia the intermediate vehicles originally housed catering galleys, but these have now been removed to provide extra passenger accommodation. An intermediate vehicle from a Midland Main Line set is illustrated. These vehicles are now operated by Arriva Cross Country.* **Author**

Left: *One of the strengths of the Adtranz and later Bombardier Turbostar build has been flexibility, especially in terms of interior design. Virtually any configuration of seating class, style, luggage stack, toilet or catering module can be inserted. The lease owners at day one stipulated flexibility as it was foreseen that a huge re-lease business would be worked by the UK railways following privatisation and each new operator would have their own desires for layout. Standard tracks are built into the aluminium frames to take the seat, luggage rack and module fixings. The seating layout shown is a standard class 2+2 arrangement for Anglia Railways; at the far end is a disabled access toilet compartment with a sliding door, allowing wheelchair entry.* **Author**

Right: *A standard design of driving cab has been fitted to all derivatives of Class 170 Turbostar. Its style when introduced set new standards for driver comfort and was designed with full agreement of the train drivers' trade unions ASLE&F and RMT. The cab uses the one controller (left hand operated) for power and brake, with a pull motion for power (throttle) and a push movement for braking. The driver's left hand also operates the master switch for direction control. All other controls and indications are provided on a wrap around style desk, with a foot-operated driver's safety device which incorporates a vigilance device. The cab illustrated is from a Class 170/2 deployed on the Anglia network (now National Express East Anglia).* **Author**

When the South Central, now Southern, franchise came to modernise its non-electric services on the Ashford-Hastings-Brighton, Oxted and Uckfield lines, Porterbrook leasing procured a fleet of Turbostar units.

Originally an order for six 2-car and six 4-car sets was placed; the two-car sets were built first and delivered to Selhurst depot as Class 170. Soon after delivery it was agreed that to provide some form of standardisation, the trains' BSI couplers should be replaced with Dellner 12 couplers, allowing emergency coupling with the operator's electric Class 377 fleet. This work was done at Selhurst by Bombardier and the sets reclassified as 171, apart from this change the sets are a Class 170.

By the time the four-car sets were delivered in 2004, Dellner couplers were fitted from new.

Fleet expansion came in 2004 when three extra sets were purpose-built at Derby and a fourth was obtained from South West Trains when they dispensed with Class 170s.

Two-car sets are formed of a Driving Motor Composite and a Driving Motor Standard, the first class area being directly behind the driving position. The four-car sets are formed of two DMC cars and two intermediate Motor Seconds, which each seat 74. All seating is provided in the 2+2 style in standard class and 2+1 in first class.

The livery applied is Southern green and white with dark green contrasting passenger doors.

Sets are allocated to purpose-built accommodation at Selhurst shed and operate specifically on the Ashford-Hastings-Brighton and London to Uckfield/Oxted lines.

Traction is provided by one MTU6R183TD engine under each vehicle using a Voith T211 final drive. The top speed is 100mph. ●

Below: *After years of travel in Class 205 (Hampshire) and Class 207 (Oxted) DEMUs, passengers on the Marshlink route between Ashford and Brighton as well as on the Oxted and Uckfield line had new levels of passenger comfort after the Class 171s were introduced from 2003. On 2 February 2008, four-car set No 171806 crosses Oxted Viaduct forming the 15.08 London Bridge to Uckfield.* **Stacey Thew**

Above: *Passenger figures on the Uckfield line usually require one of the six four-car units to be deployed on the duty. The run between Uckfield and London Bridge takes just 1hr 15min, stopping at all stations on the branch line, then East Croydon to provide a connection with Southern's coastal services and then fast to London Bridge. On 2 February 2008, set No 171806 awaits time at Crowborough with the 13.44 Uckfield to London Bridge.* **Stacey Thew**

Below: *With its first class end nearest the camera, two-car Class 171 'Turbostar' No 171721 hurries past the site of Coulsdon South station on 21 April 2006, forming the 14.08 London Bridge to Uckfield. During weekdays at off-peak times a two-car set is sufficient to cover the passenger demands of the line.*
Brian Morrison

21 Class 175

In the period immediately following the privatisation of the UK railways in the mid-1990s, a number of operators were required, either by franchise commitment or the desire to modernise their railway, to order new stock.

All of the principal builders put together detailed plans of possible designs and touted their products to the lease companies and train operators.

FirstGroup, which operated the North Western franchise as well as the Great Western franchise opted for an Alstom product for their DMU needs. The train offered was part of the Coradia 1000 range and was offered in a number of different configurations and indeed body styles.

First North Western, through Lease Company Angel Trains, ordered 11 two-car and 16 three-car sets, numbered 175001-011 and 175101-116 respectively.

The design was low-density using a mix of airline and group seats in the 2+2 style, all styled for standard class occupancy. Toilets were provided in each vehicle and the structural design used one sliding plug door at vehicle ends feeding a transverse walkway for access. Passenger saloons were separated from the vestibule by power operated sliding doors. A full-width driving cab was provided and no provision was made for end corridors. Body structures were made of steel.

The design used one underfloor-mounted Cummins N14 engine of 450hp under each vehicle driving a Voith T211 transmission.

Couplings were of the fully automatic Scharfenberg type.

Construction of the units was carried out at Alstom's Washwood Heath plant (the former Metro-Cammell facility) in Birmingham, with body structures purchased in from Mainland Europe. Fitting out commenced in early 1999 with the first complete set, No 175101, rolling off the production line for an official launch on 15 July 1999, before introduction in early 2000.

The sets were painted in FirstGroup 'swirl' livery, with the First name and logo on the cab side doors and the North Western name in the mid-body position. Sets were allocated to a new shed complex built at Chester, roughly mid-position in their intended operating range on the North Wales Coast, Blackpool and northwards to Cumbria and as far south as Birmingham and eastwards to Manchester. The facility was operated by Alstom and was purpose built for the Class 175s.

With re-mapping of the various franchises in 2003, the Class 175s and the routes operated were transferred to Wales and Borders, subsequently Arriva Trains Wales. As part of this franchise, 11 sets every day were sub-leased to First North Western and later TransPennine Express until December 2006, after which all sets were operated by Arriva Trains Wales. Under the 2003 franchise changes the sets expanded their operating range to work the north-south Wales service linking Holyhead with Cardiff.

The Arriva Trains Wales turquoise and white livery has also been applied to sets as repainting has fallen due.

When the original order was placed for the North Western three-car units it was planned to use a streamlined front end, similar to that applied to the Class 180s, but this plan was dropped during the early design process. ●

Below: *One of the driving cars for three-car set No 175102 is seen inside the main assembly hall at Alstom, Washwood Heath on 15 July 1999. In common with Metro-Cammell and Alstom practice, the shells were sourced from another factory and not formed from raw materials in the Birmingham plant. For the Class 175 build, the shells came from a sister Alstom plant in Spain and transported by road and ferry to the UK. When this view was taken only the doors and coupler had been added.* **Author**

Above: *To maintain the fleet of 70 Class 175 vehicles new purpose-built depot facilities were erected at Chester, replacing the former BR depot. Apart from the covered four-line shed and amenity block, several outside stabling sidings were provided with toilet flushing equipment and provision of general servicing needs; these were equipped with standard-height platforms for staff. Two-car sets Nos 175004 and 175005 share space in the outside stabling sidings on 4 February 2000, the day the facility was officially opened.* **Author**

Below: *Two-car set No 175009 departs through the platform pointwork at Crewe and heads towards Manchester Airport with a service from Chester on 23 March 2001. By 2001 a number of problems had befallen the fleet, but dedicated maintenance at Chester managed to return the fleet to provide a good miles per casualty figure, with reliability in recent years much improved.* **Author**

Left: *Following the franchise changes in 2003 to reflect one operator responsible for most services in Wales, with the formation of Arriva Trains Wales, the FirstGroup branding was quickly removed. However as sets were not due for a repaint the First colours remained. Three-car set No 175111 is seen in one of the north facing bays at Crewe on 29 July 2004 awaiting departure with the 14.29 to Holyhead.* **Author**

Middle: *Once the Class 175s were fully deployed on the North Wales Coast route the service was transformed into a reliable regular timetabled operation and was well accepted by the travelling public. The down side was that the route no longer had such an intense loco-hauled service using Class 37s which was not welcomed by haulage enthusiasts. On the plus side, the new timetable saw considerable passenger growth on the route to such an extend that some services were full and standing and extra resources were needed to cope with demand. On 29 July 2004, set No 175008 departs from Rhyl bound for Holyhead.* **Author**

Below: *Following the 2003 franchise changes, the Class 175s commenced working north-south Wales services linking Holyhead and the North Wales coast towns with the Welsh capital Cardiff. For the launch of this through service via Birmingham one set was painted in the standard Arriva Trains Wales turquoise livery, but the majority were just branded with Arriva markings on the body centre in the position where the original North Western name was carried. On 29 June 2004, set No 175003* Eisteddfod Genedlaethol Cymru *departs from Newport with the 09.10 Milford Haven to Manchester Piccadilly through service.* **Author**

Above: *With its bilingual bodyside branding clearly visible, FirstGroup-liveried set No 175107 departs from Newport (Gwent) on 29 June 2007 forming the 07.28 Manchester Piccadilly to Carmarthen. Since deployment on the Cardiff route it was possible between mid-2003 and February 2008 to see both the Class 175 and 180 versions of the Alstom Coradia 1000 product line side by side.* **Author**

Below: *By 2008 just two of the Arriva Trains Wales operated Class 175s had been repainted into house colours, one two-car and one three-car set. In this view the two-car unit No 175008 is seen passing Helsby on 24 January 2006, forming the 09.16 Manchester Piccadilly to Llandudno service.* **Mark Bearton**

Concurrent with the FirstGroup order for *Coradia 1000* units for their North West franchise, the company placed an order through Angel Trains for 14 five-car express High Speed DMUs with streamlined cab ends classified as 180 and identified as 'Adelante'. These were to assist with the HST fleet on semi-fast Paddington to Bristol, Cardiff, Oxford and Cotswold line services.

In keeping with the Class 175s, the body shells were produced at the Alstom plant in Spain and delivered by road to the Alstom plant in Washwood Heath, Birmingham for fitting out. One of the most complex parts of the assembly was the pre-formed glass fibre streamlined front end, which was attached to the steel body assembly after arrival in the UK.

Passenger accommodation in four vehicles, (two driving cars and two intermediates) was set out for standard class occupancy in the 2+2 open layout, using a mix of airline and group seats. One of the intermediate vehicles (coupled behind a driving car) was set out for first class travel, using 2+1 seating, with a mix of airline and group seats. Toilets were provided in each

vehicle with a small buffet in one intermediate motor standard. A small drink and food preparation area was located at one end of the first class coach.

Passenger access was by one single leaf sliding plug door at either end of each coach, feeding a transverse walkway, entry to passenger saloons was by bi-parting local operated sliding doors.

Power was provided by one Cummins QSK19 engine below each vehicle, rated at 750hp driving a hydraulic transmission. The top speed of sets was 125mph and full GW style automatic train protection was fitted.

Delivered in 2000, the sets were a major headache for the owners and operators, with numerous problems preventing the units from entering service. The national and transport media and stakeholders were first shown a set in a high-profile roll-out at London Paddington on 10 August 2000 when set No 180101 was propelled into Platform 1 by Class 47 No 47815. At the time the sets were not allowed to operate under their own power on the national network.

The first time a Class 180 formed a passenger train was on 25 July 2001 when set No 180103 formed a media special from Bristol St Philips Marsh depot to Bristol Temple Meads. Soon after this the sets were allowed into passenger service, operating on Paddington - Cardiff, Bristol, Oxford and Worcester lines. By 2004 Exeter and even Plymouth was added to the operating area, but serious problems were still apparent and with the revised First Great Western franchise from April 2006 it was announced that the sets would be phased out of service at the earliest opportunity and replaced by additional HST sets displaced by other operators. Problems included power units, transmissions, fires and parts of the bodywork falling off.

The sets continued in reduced numbers to operate until mid 2008 when sets were taken out of traffic and stored at Alstom, Oxley pending owners Angel Trains finding another customer to operate the fleet. Several possibilities exist, such as Arriva Trains and Hull Trains, but major rebuilding will be required by any operator.

The sets were painted in FGW 'Barbie' livery when built and remained thus until 2008. ●

Below: *The body shells for the Class 180s started to turn up at Alstom's Washwood Heath plant in mid-1999 and shared workshop space with the Class 175 production line. One of the biggest challenges of the project was the installation of the preformed GRP streamlined nose-cone, which had hinged panels covering the Scharfenberg coupler. An early trial fitting of a nose cone is pictured at Washwood Heath on 15 July 1999. Note several Class 175 vehicles on the left and in the background.* **Author**

Right: *Problems with the front end fittings on the Class 180s, including horn covers, lamp cluster screens and coupling box doors were always prevalent, with a number just falling off during normal service. Two sets Nos 180109 (left) and 180113 (right) are seen under the Brunel roof at Paddington on 4 March 2004, forming the 15.03 Cheltenham and 15.15 to Bristol. On both sets the horn covers are missing, while the set on the left appears to have had a replacement coupling cover devoid of number or First branding. It is interesting to note that the passengers were unable to board the train, even though the door release lights were on indicating the doors were available for use.* **Author**

Below: *To enable west of England train crews to be trained on Class 180 operation for their deployment on Paddington to Exeter and Plymouth services from the 2004 winter timetable, two weeks of driver training operated in August 2004 using the 14.35 Paddington to Plymouth service. On 2 August 2004, sets Nos 180104 and 180110 pass Aller, west of Newton Abbot forming the 14.35 Paddington to Plymouth. After deployment on West Country routes only one train on Monday to Friday operated west of Exeter and this was replaced by HST stock from 12 December 2007.* **Author**

Above: *The body style of the Class 180 was very pleasing to the eye and the design of the Great Western 'Barbie' livery suited the profile well. One unusual feature of the Class 180 driving cab was the driver's emergency exit arrangement from the cab. In case of a major problem, he was able to release and push out the body panel surrounding the cab side window and then climb out by use of a rope ladder! Set No 180106, viewed from its Standard Class end is seen at Reading forming an Oxford to Paddington service on 10 August 2006.* **Author**

Below: *Although the Class 180s only formed limited services west of Exeter, the fleet were rostered for a number of Paddington to Exeter semi-fast services, allowing more of the core InterCity services to operate with less frequent stops. On 11 April 2005, set No 180106 departs from Whiteball Tunnel and crosses from Somerset into Devon forming the 09.45 Paddington to Exeter service. Note the missing coupling cover, extended coupling and the coach number painted on the drum box of the coupler.* **Author**

Above: *Looking very stylish and perhaps more pleasing to the eye than the present FGW HST fleet, a ten-car formation of Class 180 stock formed of sets Nos 180114 and 180104 passes along the sea wall at Dawlish on 3 August 2004 forming the 14.35 Paddington to Plymouth service. The front end body lines are somewhat spoilt by the missing door over the coupling.* **Author**

Below: *The very busy London Paddington to Oxford route was always one of the strongholds of the Class 180 fleet, offering 125mph high-quality service, including first class accommodation on the one-hour-long run. On a rather cold 9 February 2007, set No 180102, devoid of coupling cover panel stands in the northbound platform at Oxford after arrival of the 08.52 Paddington to Worcester service.* **Author**

By 2003-04, Siemens had made an impressive mark in the UK rail industry with its high-quality Desiro product, supplied in both AC and DC electric forms to several operators. The company also offered the same basic modular product in an underfloor diesel-powered version.

Following the formation of the First TransPennine Express franchise, the operator was required to seek and procure new trains for use on the North East to Manchester via the Pennine route, as well as in the North West to such locations as Blackpool and the Cumbrian Coast.

Various products were examined including the ever-popular Bombardier Turbostar, but the winner of the competitive tender was Siemens, to provide 51 three-car units.

Built in Germany, the sets offer a low-density 2+2 interior for standard class and 2+1 for first class travellers. Toilets are provided in two of the three vehicles.

The sets are only corridor-fitted within each set, but provide accommodation for 15 first and 154 standard class passengers per set.

Traction is provided by an underslung Cummins OSK19 engine set to deliver 750hp under each coach, driving a Voith hydraulic transmission. The top speed of sets is 100mph.

Passenger accommodation is fed by two pairs of sliding plug doors on each side of each vehicle, a separate crew sliding door is provided in the cab position.

Delivered to the UK via the Channel Tunnel in 2005-06 the units are allocated to purpose-built depot facilities at Ardwick, Manchester. Additional servicing facilities have also been built at York and Cleethorpes; all are operated by Siemens on a train life maintenance contract.

The Class 185s entered service progressively from 14 March 2006 and were well accepted by passengers and staff. On delivery to the UK sets were painted in FirstGroup blue, onto which the standard 'Dynamic Lines' branding has been applied.

A major expansion to the Class 185 network occurred with the franchise changes in December 2007, when First TransPennine Express took over the Manchester Airport to Edinburgh/Glasgow service from Virgin Trains.

Growth expectancy on all FPTE routes is likely to see the present fleet of three-car sets unable to cope with traffic demands and it is expected that Government announcements of extra rolling stock will see 51 extra Motor Standards built to augment each set to four coaches. ●

Below: *The Class 185 fleet has a wide operating range, spreading from Newcastle and Edinburgh in the North East to the Cumbrian Coast via Manchester and onwards to Glasgow in the North West. On 9 April 2007, set No 185116 traverses the Windemere branch between Staveley and Burneside, forming the 11.37 from Windemere to Manchester Airport.* **Brian Morrison**

Right: *First TransPennine Express No 185139 rounds the curve at Newton Hall, Durham on 10 September 2007 forming a Manchester Airport to Newcastle express service.* **Ken Short**

Middle: *The two driving cars of the Class 185 are of different structural design, reflecting the different interior layout. With its DMS car leading, which has normal position windows, set No 185148 awaits departure from Manchester Piccadilly bound for Manchester Airport on 16 September 2007.* **Stacey Thew**

Below: *The First Class driving car has solid bodywork between the first pair of passenger doors and the driving cab, as seen in this view of set No 185125 at Sheffield on 14 August 2006, working the 15.57 Manchester Airport to Cleethorpes duty.* **Brian Morrison**

Above: *One of the principal locations to see and photograph Class 185 stock is Doncaster. On 13 February 2007 FTPE Nos 185112 and 185117 depart from Doncaster, forming the 10.52 from Manchester Airport to Cleethorpes and the 11.28 from Cleethorpes to Manchester Airport.* **Brian Morrison**

Left: *An area which has seen considerable development in recent years has been Leeds, with the station totally rebuilt to accommodate enhanced services on the East Coast, West Yorkshire PTE, CrossCountry and First TransPennine Express corridors. At peak times a train arrives/departs Leeds City every minute! On 16 December 2006, set No 185142 slows for the Leeds station stop with a Manchester to Newcastle via Leeds and York service.* **Brian Garrett**

Right: *The Class 185s operate through some superb scenery over the Diggle route, which in crossing the Pennines, offers some excellent photographic locations - as long as the weather is good. On 29 June 2006, set No 185119 passes Diggle forming train 1K11, the 10.39 Hull to Manchester Piccadilly. Services on this FTPE corridor have now been taken over by Class 170s.*
Mark Bearton

At the time of Virgin Trains' win of the CrossCountry franchise, the commitment was made to replace the entire existing fleet of trains, which ranged from loco-hauled Mk2 formations to HST stock. The original CrossCountry management team dictated the train design and after much deliberation whether to opt for a total DMU-based fleet or a split between loco-hauled and DMUs, opted for a DMU design.

The specification went out to competitive tender and Bombardier Transportation won the contract.

In a mis-led belief that new shorter four- and five car trains could replace 8-10 car HST and Mk2 formations, a fleet of 74 'Voyager' diesel-electric units were ordered. In the consideration that tilting trains could save time on the CrossCountry route (between Oxford and Birmingham and on the northern section of the West Coast) a split fleet of Voyagers were constructed, 34 four-car non-tilt sets classified as 220 and 44 tilting units classified as 221, of which order 40 sets were of five-car formation and the final four 4-car formation.

Assembly of the sets was split between the Bombardier factories in Bruges, Belgium and Wakefield, England, with assembly commencing at the Bruges site in early 2000 and the first non-tilt set No 220001 emerging for testing on 18 October 2000. Static testing was carried out at Bruges followed by dynamic testing in the Bruges-Oostende area. Production of the sets was rapid and an introduction to service at first on the Reading to Birmingham line came on 21 May 2001.

It soon became apparent that the Voyager sets were totally inadequate in terms of passenger accommodation and huge problems surrounded overcrowding. In some cases this was answered by running a more frequent service, but this was not sustainable on the failing Network Rail system. Double sets were used on some routes, but Virgin Trains' ambition to launch Operation Princess, transforming the ageing and dilapidated 'Cinderella' CrossCountry to a 'Princess' network in late September 2002 failed, with the network unable to cope with the demands of extra trains on a modified route structure, and it was not long before a number of

routes were abandoned and massive changes made to the service plan.

The Class 220 and 221 fleets were allocated to a new large purpose-built Bombardier depot at Central Rivers near Burton-on-Trent where virtually all levels of maintenance could be carried out, satellite maintenance facilities were set up throughout the network.

The Voyager fleet was set out for 2+2 accommodation in standard class and 2+1 in first, however by virtue of the design being suitable for tilt operation, the body profile narrowed at the top and degraded the passenger environment. First class accommodation was provided on one driving car, while the rest of the train was for standard class use. A small shop (buffet) was located in one intermediate vehicle and a small catering area was located directly behind the driving cab in the first class vehicle.

Entry to vehicles was by a single-leaf sliding plug door feeding a transverse walkway with bi-parting sliding doors into the passenger compartments. Luggage space was very limited on the design, the above-seat racks were too small for anything but a handbag and coat and

Below: *Fabrication of all 352 Voyager coaches were carried out in the Bombardier plant in Bruges, Belgium, with shells for UK-built sets transported by road to Wakefield. At the height of the build, anything up to 40 body shells could be found at the Belgian factory at any one time. A driving car for a Class 220 set is seen in the early stages of fabrication.* **Author**

insufficient luggage stacks were provided throughout the train; after a short time some seats were removed to provide extra luggage accommodation.

All sets were painted in Virgin Trains silver and red livery, offset by a yellow warning end and black cab-window surround.

Apart from the ongoing overcrowding problems, many operational problems befell the fleet; the most public of which was of seawater ingress into roof-mounted electrical boxes when traversing the South Devon sea wall at Dawlish and Teignmouth at times of rough seas. Several sets failed completely and had to be dragged away with massive delays to passengers. Modifications to the electrics solved the problem, but not before great damage was done to the Virgin name and the Voyager brand.

The vast majority of the Voyager fleet was operated on the CrossCountry network, but a handful worked with the Virgin West Coast function to work over the North Wales Coast.

The Voyager fleet remained intact until re-mapping of the rail franchises was announced, which saw the CrossCountry franchise removed from Virgin Trains control from November 2007 and pass to Arriva Trains. As part of the franchise change sufficient Voyager sets to operate the new franchise were transferred to the new operator; this saw all members of Class 220 and 28 members of the Class 221 tilting fleet transfer to the new operator, while Virgin West Coast retained sets Nos 221101-113/142-144 for its expanded West Coast function in the Birmingham - North West area.

Arriva Cross Country re-liveried one set, No 220017, for its official launch, and has subsequently re-branded the Virgin red and silver livery with XC Cross Country labelling.

Recognition of the non-tilt and tilting fleets of Class 220 and 221 is best achieved by reference to the bogies. The non-tilt version uses a skeleton frame bogie which appears to be rather flimsy, while the tilting sets use a more conventional heavyweight bogie.

Each vehicle within a Voyager is powered using a Cummins 750hp engine powering an electric transmission. ●

Top: *Viewed from its inner end, a driving car for use in a Class 220 set is seen in the main assembly bay in Bruges. Behind are two intermediate vehicles with the main welding booth in the background.* **Author**

Middle: *Set No 220001 (formed of various vehicles from sets 001, 003 and 004) was officially handed over to Virgin in a ceremony at Bombardier Bruges on 6 December 2000 when a special 14.35 Bruges to Oostende was worked, seen passing Varssenaere, one of the rare occasions a UK train has operated in passenger service in Belgium.* **Author**

Right: *The Voyager sets painted in Virgin Trains red and silver livery always looked very eye-catching and were largely accepted well by the public. On 2 September 2004, set No 220028 passes the long closed station of Brent in Devon forming the 12.25 Plymouth to Glasgow.* **Author**

Above: *For the transfer of the Cross Country franchise from Virgin Trains to Arriva, one set, No 220017 was re-branded in the new colours and entered service on franchise change day, 11 November 2007. Most other XC operated sets were just branded with the CrossCountry name and full repainting will take place when this is due in the long term maintenance plan. On 8 February 2008, set No 220017 departs from Newton Abbot, forming the 10.24 Manchester Piccadilly to Plymouth service.* **Stacey Thew**

Left: *With a total of 3,000hp available to a four-car set and 3,750hp on a five-car formation, acceleration from a stand has always been rapid and hill climbing made easy. With a top speed of 125mph, the Voyager fleet has provided some very spirited running and without 'black box' OTMR systems it is often wondered just how fast a Voyager would be able to travel! Heading out of Devon and into Somerset at Whiteball on 6 April 2006, set No 220011 forms the 10.48 Exeter St Davids to Newcastle service, with its first class driving car at the rear of the formation.* **Author**

Second Generation DMUs

Above: *When Virgin Trains introduced the Voyager train fleet, the marketing and press teams did a superb job in spreading the word, holding high profile press events in many towns, which frequently involved twinning a Class 220 with a specific location, an event bound to get local coverage. One such event was held at Llandudno station on 23 November 2002 when set No 220008 was named* Draig Gymreig/Welsh Dragon. *The set is seen approaching the town station on a special run from Llandudno Junction.* **Author**

Below: *With Virgin Trains it was always rare to find two five-car sets working in multiple. This was not favoured due to platform lengths, and frequently eight- or nine-car formations were the norm on peak trains or busy days. Here a nine-car formation of sets Nos 220023 and 221123 pull off the Paignton branch at Aller, west of Newton Abbot on 4 September 2004 forming the 17.35 Paignton to Manchester Piccadilly.* **Author**

Above: *Assembly of the Class 221 'Super Voyager' tilting sets was shared between the Bruges and Wakefield factories of Bombardier Transportation. Seen towards the end of the production cycle, the five vehicles for set No 221139 are seen in the Wakefield fitting-out area. The near clinical conditions in which modern trains are constructed are a far cry from the workshops of just a couple of generations ago.* **Author**

Below: *Following construction of the first tilting set in Bruges a major dynamic test period followed with numerous runs in Belgium and France. The major tilting tests were carried out on the line between Brive and Cahors in France, where previous tilting trials had been undertaken. On 1 February 2002 a small group of UK railway media was taken by Virgin Trains to the line and witnessed set No 221101 being put through its tilt testing, later travelling on the set from Cahors to Brive-le-Gaillarde. Super Voyager No 221101 departs from Brive-le-Gaillarde and overtakes SNCF BB No BB7262 forming the 16.17 to Paris Austerlitz.* **Author**

Above: *To identify a standard non-tilt and tilting Voyager different-coloured Virgin cast logos were attached to the front ends. Red indicated a tilting Voyager and silver a non-tilt. To assist passengers and staff in identifying the first class end of the train, a yellow coupling cover was applied at the first class end, located directly above the Dellner coupler. Set No 221133 awaits departure of the 06.40 Plymouth to Newcastle under the great roof at York station on 20 July 2004.* **Author**

Below: *The Voyager stock when painted in Virgin CrossCountry livery always looked pleasing to the eye, with the silver and red suiting the body profile. The 10.36 Birmingham New Street-Glasgow Central service is seen at speed passing Plumpton, south of Carlisle, on 9 April 2007, formed of Class 221 'Super Voyager' No 221134 Mary Kingsley.* **Brian Morrison**

Above: *The fitting of a full tilt mechanism to the 44 Super Voyager sets was a very expensive extra when it is considered just how much time can be saved on the West Coast Main Line and over the short tilt section on the Oxford to Birmingham route. With the new Arriva franchise not operating north of Birmingham one wonders if the equipment will be kept fully commissioned. Working over the East Coast main line on its racing section north of York, set No 221119 passes Shipton-on-Benningborough on 1 July 2004 forming a Newcastle to Plymouth service.* **Author**

Left: *Major changes were introduced to the Cross Country operating routes from November 2007, with Cross Country services from the South West now all travelling to the North East and Scotland, meaning that Cross Country customers from the far west to Preston, Carlisle and Glasgow now have to change trains in Birmingham - a move not welcomed by passengers. On a beautiful 23 April 2004 day, Super Voyager No 221114 approaches Derby at Duffield with an Edinburgh to Plymouth via York service. Note the first or club class yellow band on the coupling cover, indicating that the DMF car was leading.* **Author**

Second Generation DMUs

Above: *Maintenance for the entire fleet of Class 220 and 221 sets is carried out at the purpose-built depot complex at Central Rivers near Burton-on-Trent. This depot was originally only used by the Virgin Trains-operated sets, but following introduction of similar trains on Midland Main Line and Hull Trains, these sets have also received attention at the depot. From November 2007 the depot became the principal base for the Arriva Cross Country operation, but was still responsible for the remaining Virgin Trains-operated sets. Temporarily formed as a five-car set, the final member of the Class 221 fleet, No 221144, is seen inside the lifting shop at Central Rivers on 14 October 2002.* **Author**

Below: *From the November 2007 franchise changes, the CrossCountry business no longer operates north of Manchester over the West Coast Main Line; this route is now the domain of Virgin West Coast using Class 390 'Pendolino' stock. On 29 September 2005, five-car 'Super Voyager' No 221139* Leif Erikson *heads south through the magnificent countryside at Crawford in the Clyde Valley.* **Chris Perkins**

Following construction of the Class 220 and 221 sets for Virgin Trains, further very similar train sets were ordered by HSBC Rail for use on Midland Mainline and Hull Trains. Classified 222, these are diesel-electric multiple units suitable for high-speed running at up to 125mph. The 27 sets were manufactured by Bombardier Transportation at Bruges in Belgium. Speculation exists that further units of the design could be ordered.

Although similar to the Class 220 and 221 units used by Arriva and Virgin Trains, and having a similar appearance, the Class 222 has a radically different interior, upgraded after lessons were learned from the Class 220 and 221 which received negative feedback regarding cramped conditions. The Class 222s have more components fitted under vehicles.

Two distinct breeds of Class 222 exist, those operated with Stagecoach East Midlands Trains and those with FirstGroup's Hull Trains division.

The East Midlands Trains fleet was delivered to the previous franchise operator, Midland Main Line, and sets were formed in four- and nine-car formations. After a short time of operating experience it was agreed to reform the nine-car sets to eight vehicles and strengthen seven of the four-car sets to five-vehicle formation.

The four car sets are formed Driving Motor First seating 22 and Motor Composite seating 28 first and 22 standard, a Motor Standard Buffet seating 62 standard and a Driving Standard seating 40 standard. The nine-car sets, designed for long distance work and provided with extra first class catering in the first class driving car seated a total of 106 first and 372 standard, but after size reduction now only accommodate 304 standard passengers. The augmenting of the four-car sets to five increased the seating on a unit to 50 first and 192 standard, more in keeping with traffic demands on the London St Pancras-Sheffield/Nottingham route.

Standard class seating is provided in the 2+2 style in a mix of group and airline configuration, while the first class seating is set out in the 2+1 style.

Single-leaf sliding plug doors are located at the ends of each vehicle and feed a transverse walkway, from which access doors give entry into the passenger saloons.

The exterior design of the Class 222 is very similar to Class 220 and 221, but slight differences exist in the door/window positions, front under coupling skirt and the cab end body contour.

When introduced sets were finished in Midland Mainline turquoise and white with yellow warning ends. Following the transfer of the franchise to East Midlands Trains their distinctive white, blue and red colour scheme has been applied.

Under the Midland Mainline operation, the Class 222 sets became known as 'Meridian' units.

The final four Class 222s to roll off the Bombardier production line were for Hull Trains, a company which operates a limited service on the Hull to London King's Cross route and which started life using Class 170 stock. The business soon outgrew these trains and replacements were sought and found in a small fleet of four Class 222s which became known as 'Pioneers'. The four sets are formed Driving Motor First with buffet, two Motor Standards, one with a small buffer and one Driving Motor Standard. Seating is provided for 22 first and 170 standard class passengers in the 2+2 and 2+1 seating style. The sets are finished in a grey and green livery style and based at Crofton depot. One set (No 222103) met with a serious accident at Crofton in 2007 which wrote off two vehicles, and at the time of writing only three sets remain in traffic. ●

Below: *Formed as a four-car set, Midland Mainline unit No 222013 (now a five-car unit) stands in the temporary MML platforms at St Pancras International on 6 July 2006 awaiting departure with the 10.00 semi-fast service to Derby. Soon after this image was taken, these platforms closed and new permanent MML facilities on the opposite side of the station opened. These platforms will soon become the South Eastern high-speed Kentlink terminal.* **Author**

Above: *With the world-famous Brush Traction plant on the right side, the 14.07 Nottingham to London St Pancras slows for the Loughborough station stop on 3 May 2007, formed of unit No 222011, one of the five-vehicle formations modified in 2006 by inserting one Motor Standard from the original nine-car Class 222 formations.* **Brian Morrison**

Right: *The full introduction of the nine-car Class 222s was a drawn-out affair with the then operator Midland Mainline and the Department for Transport in a wrangle over the lease agreement due to changes within the franchise between the time the stock was ordered and ready for service. The nine-car sets, however, did not remain in traffic for very long before a reformation programme was launched to remove one MS from each set and strengthen a like number of four-car sets to five vehicle formation. Nine-car set No 222004 passes Cossington on 2 June 2006 forming train 1F38, the 15.25 London St Pancras to Sheffield.* **Mark Bearton**

Above: *It is amazing what a coat of paint (or application of new vinyl) can do for a train. For the official launch of Stagecoach East Midlands Trains on 12 November 2007, five-car set No 222017 was re-branded in the new colours in an amazing 'make-over' at Central Rivers depot. The EMT livery is based on South West Trains colours and the swirl end to the driving cars suits the body profile of the vehicles. EMT has maintained the identification of the first class end of the train by the application of yellow to the electrical connection box of the auto-coupler. Set No 222017 is seen at St Pancras International on 12 November 2007.* **Author**

Left: *First class accommodation on the East Midlands Trains Class 222s is laid out in the 2+1 style in a mix of airline and group seats. All seats have a fixed table for work or catering purposes. Power points are provided for laptop computers or phone charging. Seats all have hinged armrests, curtains are provided and windows have pull-down blinds. The interior of set No 222012 is shown.* **Author**

Above and Below: *Five-car set No 222017 stands at Nottingham station on 12 November 2007, the first weekday of the new East Midlands franchise and the first public showing of the new livery. The set is viewed from its DMS end, and the quality of the vinyl application is very apparent. A few years ago such a re-livery would have seen the bodywork rubbed down and primer, undercoat and top coats applied; today, through the clever application of plastic film, quite stunning graphics and angles can be obtained which would have been difficult in paint. The view below, ideal for modellers, shows the position of bodyside branding and decals, such as disabled-access, overhead-power-line and sliding-door danger signs, together with vehicle numbering and yellow lifting points on a clean vehicle body. The black oblong to the right on both passenger doors is a route and service display, giving the train details, train number and next station call.*
Both: **Author**

Above: *The Hull Trains operation, a part of FirstGroup and one of the growing number of open access operators, started off operating a London King's Cross to Hull service with a fleet of hired-in Anglia Class 170s. Soon a dedicated fleet of three-car sets with enhanced interiors were provided to the operator, and in 2005 these were replaced by four purpose-built Class 222 sets, known by the operator as 'Pioneers'. On 11 April 2006, set No 222101* Professor George Gray *stands under the trainshed roof at London King's Cross awaiting departure as the 12.10 to Hull.* **Brian Morrison**

Below: *With a top speed of 125mph, these Class 222s have been authorised to operate over the fast tracks of the East Coast Main Line and do not interfere with the principal East Coast operator. The 12.10 Hull Trains service to Hull departs from London King's Cross on 12 May 2006, formed of set No 222104* Sir Terry Farrell. **Brian Morrison**

Second Generation DMUs

Above: *In spring 2007 disaster struck the Hull Trains operation when one of their sets, No 222103, was involved in a very serious incident while undergoing maintenance at Bombardier's Crofton depot. The set, supported on synchronised lifting jacks, fell to the ground after failure of one of the jacks. Two vehicles were seriously damaged and the set stored. To provide cover for services, Hull Trains hired-in a loco-hauled formation powered by preserved Class 86 No 86101. In better days, set No 222103* Dr John Godber *passes Alexandra Palace on 20 November 2006, forming the 10.11 Hull to London King's Cross.*
Brian Morrison

Below: *After diverging from the main East Coast route at Doncaster, the Hull Trains services pass through North Humberside and in places these state-of-the-art units are working through semaphore signalled areas, such as here at Crabley Creek near Brough, where on 4 July 2006 set No 222101 forms the 12.10 London King's Cross to Hull.* **Mark Bearton**

Few second-generation DMU vehicles have entered departmental or service stock status, mainly as they are too young and largely still in front line service.

The Class 210 development DEMUs saw three of its vehicles pass to the departmental board. The two motor coaches Nos 60200 (53000) and 60201 (53001) were destined to become an Amey Railways track inspection train. They were allocated the departmental numbers 977649/650 (which they carried on NSE-branded blue and grey livery), and were allocated track inspection vehicle numbers 999604 and 999603. Neither vehicle was converted, both being stored at Eastleigh Works for many years before being broken up by contractor Raxstar in May 2003.

One vehicle of special interest was the Trailer Composite from the four-car Class 210 set No 60450 (58000); after the Class 210 had finished its main-line development work on the Western region and it was returned to the Engineering Development Unit at Derby, the coach was taken into departmental stock by the BR Research and Development arm and renumbered RDB977645.

Within the RTC's advanced vehicles laboratory the coach was rebuilt as a trial 'All Electric Vehicle', removing all pneumatic systems from the coach, such as brakes and door control equipment. This was carried out as part of a development for the Advanced Multiple Unit which was projected to have no on-board air systems, with all functions controlled by electric.

A special brake system was installed and at least two pairs of exterior passenger doors were refitted with an electric system. Some internal equipment was also tested including toilet compartment items.

The coach did venture out on the main line on one or two occasions marshalled within consists of other test cars, but the majority of development and testing work was carried out with various contractors within the confines of the Railway Technical Centre.

The most celebrated second-generation DMU in Departmental service is the Class 150/1-outline Track Assessment Unit formed of vehicles 999600 and 999601. These were purpose-built vehicles constructed at BREL York works as part of the Class 150 building project in 1987 and transferred as shells to the RTC Derby for installation of sophisticated track testing equipment.

One vehicle has standard Class 150/1 body lines and is largely used as a staff support coach. The vehicle has a full width driving cab, transverse walkway behind with hinged exterior doors and a near normal seating saloon with two pairs of power-operated bi-parting sliding doors on each side.

The other vehicle was a special fabrication, being a mobile laboratory, the body sides had no automatic doors and were largely solid. A pair of hinged equipment bay doors are provided towards the inner end. This coach has a normal full width driving cab and transverse walkway behind.

When first introduced the set was painted in BR blue/grey livery offset by a broad red band at waist height, onto which the branding 'Track Recording Unit' was applied in white.

Now operated by Network Rail, the twin set is painted in yellow livery.

The front end has conventional BSI couplers but sports RTC-style jumpers on the outer ends and from time to time, depending on the test programme being undertaken, end-mounted cameras are fitted.

Under the TOPS classification system the set is classified as 950 and allocated the number 950001.

It is allocated to the Railway Technical Centre, Derby and travels the length and breadth of the UK rail network on a frequent basis. ●

Below: *The prototype 'All Electric Vehicle' No RDB977645, modified from the Class 210 TC vehicle is seen at the RTC Derby on 5 August 1992. Once the equipment development and testing had been completed, the coach was spare at the RTC and was disposed of in a clear-out of unwanted assets in 1995. It was sold to Euro Metal Recycling at Attercliffe, Sheffield and broken up in January 1996.* **Author**

Above and Below: *The purpose-built Class 150/1 outline Track Recording Unit formed of vehicles DB999600 and 999601 is a frequent sight all over the national network, operating on most lines on an annual basis and the more heavily used sections more frequently. The picture above, taken on 22 March 1994 shows the set painted in its BR blue and grey livery off-set by a red waist height band at Glasgow Queen Street awaiting departure for Fort William. This view is taken from the instrumentation or laboratory coach. Note the plug-in high intensity headlight on the front end. The view below shows the train in its present guise, painted and branded in Network Rail yellow livery. This view is from the seating coach end, which is basically a standard Class 150/1 vehicle. Over the years a number of different end fittings have been carried, in this view passing Dawlish on 5 May 2007 a camera and lighting unit is attached. Both:* **Author**

27 Second Generation DMUs

Class	Formation	Number Range	Number Built	Introduced	Builder	Owner/Operator
Railbus	DM	LEV1 (RDB975874)	1	1979	Leyland/BREL	BR Research/BR
Railbus	DM	R3/LEV3 (RDB977020)	1	1981	Leyland/BREL	BREL/Leyland/BR
Railbus	DM	LEV2	1	1980	D. Wickham	FRA (America) (Test in UK)
Railbus	DM	RB002/BREL75	1	1985	Leyland/BREL	Trials in Canada/US
Railbus	DM	RB004	1	1984	BREL	Trials in US
139 (on order)	DM	139001-02	2	2009	Parry	Porterbrook/LM
140	DMS+DMS	140001	1	1981	BREL	BR
141	DMS+DMS	141001-020/141101-120	20	1983/4	Leyland/BREL	BR
142	DMS+DMS	142001-096	96	1985-87	Leyland/BREL	BR now Angel Trains/FGW, AW, NO
143	DMS+DMS	143001-025/143601-625	25	1985-86	Alexander/Barclay	BR now Porterbrook & Private FGW, AW
144	DMS+DMS	144001-013	13	1986-87	Alexander/BREL	BR now Porterbrook/NO
144	DMS+MS+DMS	144014-023	10	1986-88	Alexander/BREL	BR now Porterbrook/NO
150/0	DMS+MS+DMSL	150001-002	2	1984-85	BREL York	BR now Angel Trains/LM
150/1	DMS+DMSL	150101-150	50	1985-86	BREL York	BR now Angel Trains/LM, TfL, FGW, NO
150/2	DMS+DMSL	150201-285	85	1987	BREL York	BR now Angel Trains and Porterbrook/NO, AW, LM, FGW
151	DMS+MS+DMSL	151001-002	2	1985-86	Metro-Cammell	BR
153	DMSL	153301-335/351-385	70	1991-92	Hunslet Barclay	BR now Angel Trains and Porterbrook/AW, EMT, NO, FGW, NEEA, LM
154 (ex 150)	DMS+MS+DMSL	154001	1	1987	BREL	BR
155	DMS+DMSL	155301-335	35	1987-88	Leyland	BR (modified to 153)
155/1	DMS+DMSL	155341-347	7	1988	Leyland	WYPTE now WY/NO
156	DMS+DMSL	156401-514	114	1987-1989	Metro-Cammell	BR now Porterbrook and Angel Trains/EMT, NEEA, NO, FSR
158/0	DMS+(MS)+DMS(DMC)	158701-872	172	1989-1992	BREL	BR now Porterbrook and Angel Trains/FSR, FGW, NO, EMT, AW, SWT

Left: The standard Network SouthEast livery, as applied to the 22 Class 159s when first introduced, looked very smart, and surprisingly the white roofs stayed very clean considering exhaust blow down. On 3 August 1996, sets Nos 159016 and 159011 depart from the Dawlish station stop forming the 09.50 Paignton to Waterloo service. **Author**

Right: *One of the driving cars for Class 158 set No 158727 is seen in the yard at Derby Litchurch Lane works on 4 May 1990, parked under the water spray arch. This device sprayed water over the vehicle structure at high pressure and from all angles to prove no leaks existed in the seals of the structure. At this time in the assembly process it was unusual to find vehicles in base aluminium at such an advanced stage of assembly, usually by the time the cab ends were applied and glazing complete the exterior two-pack paint finish was applied.* **Author**

Right Below: *The short-lived Leyland Class 155 fleet operating for Provincial as two-car sets saw the majority of units working from Cardiff on either West of England, Manchester/Liverpool or South Coast services. Set No 155322 stops at Fareham on 9 May 1990 forming a Cardiff to Portsmouth Harbour service, while on the left Class 442 'Wessex Electric' No 442409 formed the 15.35 'Solent Link' launch train to Waterloo.* **Author**

Abbreviations used in Table

AW - Arriva Trains Wales
BR - British Rail
BoS - Bank of Scotland
CR - Chiltern Railways
FRA - Federal Railroad Administration
FSR - First ScotRail
FTPE - First TransPennine Express
EMT - East Midlands Trains
FGW - First Great Western
HT - Hull Trains
LM - London Midland
NEEA - National Express East Anglia
NO - Northern
SR - Southern
SWT - South West Trains
TfL - Transport for London
WYPTE - West Yorkshire Passenger
  Transport Executive
XC - Arriva Cross Country

158/9	DMS+DMSL	158901-910	10	1991	BREL	BR/WYPT, now WT/NO
159/0	DMSL+MSL+DMCL	159001-022	22	1992	BREL	BR now Porterbrook/SWT
159/1	DMSL+MSL+DMCL	159101-108	8	(1991) 2007	(BREL) Wabtec	Porterbrook/SWT
165	DMCL+(MS)+DMSL	165001-039/101-137	76	1991-1993	BREL York	BR now Angel Trains/CR, FGW
166	DMCL+MS+DMCL	166201-221	21	1993	BREL York	BR now Angel Trains/FGW
168	DMSL+MSL+MSL+DMSL	168001-006/106-113/214-219	19	1998-2004	Bombardier Derby	Porterbrook/CR
170	DMSL+(MSL)+DMCL	170101-639	122	1998-2006	AdTranz/Bombardier Derby	Porterbrook, & HSBC/XC, NEEA, FTPE, FSR, LM
171	DMSL+(MS)+DMCL	171721-730/801-806	16	2003-2005	Bombardier Derby	Porterbrook/SR
172 (on order)	DMSL+DMSL	172211-231/331-345	27	2010	Bombardier Derby	Porterbrook/LM
175	DMSL+(MSL)+DMSL	175001-011/101-116	27	1999-2000	Alstom	Angel Trains/AW
180	DMSL+MFL+MSL+MSLB+DMS	180101-114	14	2000-2002	Alstom	Angel Trains/(off lease)
185	DMCL+MSL+DMS	185101-151	51	2005-2007	Siemens	Angel Trains/FTPE
210	DMS+(TC)+TS+DTS	210001-002	2	1981-1982	BREL York/Derby	BR
220	MSL+MSLB+MSL+MFL	220001-034	34	2000-2001	Bombardier	BoS/XC
221	MSL+MSLB+MSL+(MSL)+MFL	221101-144	44	2001-2002	Bombardier	BoS/Virgin, XC
222/1	DMF+MS+MS+DMS	222101-104	4	2005	Bombardier	HSBC/HT
222/4 & 9	DMF+MF+MF+MS+MS+MS+DMS - various	222001-023	23	2004-2005	Bombardier	HSBC/EMT

Two-car Network SouthEast 'Thames Turbo' No 165120 departs from Acton Main Line on 24 June 1994 forming the 10.48 Reading to London Paddington stopping service. **Author**